C000193755

# GOOD HONES

## THE STORY OF A MIDLANDS DYNASTY
## MARK YOUNG

MITCHELLS&BUTLERS

PALE & MILD ALES

LICENSED VICTUALLERS
BANQUET

"THE TRADE."

# GOOD HONEST BEER

## THE STORY OF A MIDLANDS DYNASTY
## MARK YOUNG

Copyright © 2011 R M YOUNG

First published in 2011 by
BROAD STREET PUBLISHING

All rights reserved. No part of this publication may be reproduced, stored in a retrieval system, or transmitted in any form or by any means without the prior written permission of the publisher, nor to be otherwise circulated in any form of binding or cover other than that in which it is published and without a similar condition being imposed on the subsequent purchaser.

ISBN 978-0-9557019-7-9

Printed and bound in Great Britain by
Short Run Press Limited, Exeter

BROAD STREET PUBLISHING
Arden Cottage, Coombeshead Road, Highweek,
Newton Abbot TQ12 1PZ
Tel +44 (0) 1626 365478

# DEDICATION

I dedicate this book to the men and women of Cape Hill Brewery, 1878-2002.

I honour the memory of William Waters Butler, Chairman of Mitchells & Butlers 1914-1939.

ACKNOWLEDGEMENTS

I thank everybody who has taken the time to reply to emails, written letters, talked over the phone and met me on my visits to Birmingham. I must thank in particular, Vernon Fisher. Vernon has been a constant source of information and we have spent several days together rummaging around M&B: and he finally got me back on the beer at The Old Swan on the 21st June! Thanks are also due to Hazel Fisher. I'll never forget my first cuppa out of the special M&B mug.

Thanks to Emma Molland, Debra Sillence and Martin Thomas who in their very different ways have contributed to this book.

I thank O C Darby for his hospitality one day in March 2011 and for his thoughts and observations on M&B. His story of The Abbey is surely the stuff of legend!

Carol Bradshaw of Persimmon has been kind and helpful. She arranged for me to launch this book at Cape Hill.

Mention must be made of the help I received from Aston Villa FC, Bedford Libraries, Birmingham Libraries, The National Archive, The Royal Regiment of Fusiliers (Warwickshire), The Smethwick Heritage Centre (where I met Christine Round, Graham Hingley and Gordon Ratherham) and The War Office.

My aunt, Pop, Owen Butler's surviving daughter, and my sister, Sarah, have been most supportive. I hope it has been worthwhile.

And, of course, this book is for Chrissie, my wife, who has lived with William Butler, Henry Mitchell et al for over five years. Her attention to detail, editing skills, encouragement, interest, love and patience are all appreciated, and she discovered where we could hang the very large portrait of Sir William in our Devon home.

# CONTENTS

ILLUSTRATIONS

All photos, unless otherwise stated, are and remain the property of the author. I have attempted to recognize all copyrights: on occasion this has been unsuccessful and I will be delighted to correct any omission. The Smethwick Heritage Centre own the copyright for the pictures from Fifty Years of Brewing and these are acknowledged as M&B/SHC: any other M&B pictures are acknowledged as M&B

COLOUR ILLUSTRATIONS PAGES 33-40

## BLACK & WHITE ILLUSTRATIONS PAGES 65-80

## COLOUR ILLUSTRATIONS PAGES 97-104

BLACK & WHITE ILLUSTRATIONS PAGES 129-144

# GOOD HONEST BEER

## A PERSONAL NOTE

When I started researching this book my knowledge of Birmingham was minimal, to the extent that I had never even heard of Broad Street. My first visit to the city proper was in 2005 when I was still a bookshop proprietor in North Devon. My shop address then was 17 Broad Street, South Molton and my publishing company was named Broad Street Publishing.

This happy coincidence only registered with me after parking in Birmingham one morning before going in search of The Crown Brewery, which still stands in reduced form in Broad Street.

My first visit followed my acquisition of a portrait of Sir William Waters Butler which had hung in my mother's various homes throughout my life. After her death it was agreed with my widely dispersed relatives that I should look after it. Looking at the portrait of my great-grandfather noting how alike we looked, I realized I actually knew very little of the man who had left money for my education and whose final Trust had bequeathed me sums of money throughout my adult life. I decided I would like to find out more about him. I can remember standing opposite The Crown that morning, digesting the link between my past and present, and decided there and then to research his past and that of the company he served for so much of his life.

GOOD HONEST BEER

INTRODUCTION

When you have lost your inns, drown your empty selves
For you will have lost the last of England

Hilaire Belloc

Good Ale is the true and proper drink of the Englishman

George Borrow

For Ale are we famous, clear wholesome and strong
One drop of it now would enliven my song.
Had my mother's milk tasted like it, I vow
I ne'er would have left, but kept suckling till now.

From Birmingham Ale, a ballad by John Freeth

This is a book predominantly about one enterprise, Mitchells &
Butlers and some of the people who created it, worked for it, and
consumed its products. At the same time I have attempted to place the
story of the company as part of a greater whole. So there are chapters
on those areas which I perceive as relevant to why M&B ever existed,
why it was such a successful company and, of course, why it
eventually ceased to function in anything like its original form. I have
tried to mix the story with a blend of hard fact, some lighter moments
and personal observation.

The temperance movement will be mentioned from time to time in
this book and forms an integral part of the story. I have seen the
results of alcohol abuse at close, domestic quarters but at the age of
60 earnestly believe that a properly run pub is a vital part of many
thousands of communities and despair of the wanton destruction by
recent governments of so much of this magnificent tradition. It is
obviously a matter for debate, but was there ever a golden age for
pubs? By this I mean not a time when brewers and publicans were

making the most money, but when the pub, as a focal point in its community, was a place where folk of all ages and types mixed together, enjoyed each other's company and drank reasonably. In recent times drinking hours have been totally relaxed with 24 hour opening now permitted. The theory behind this legislation was that by creating a 'café culture' drinking would be spread out more evenly and drunkenness would thereby diminish. In fact some city centres have become no go areas for anyone other than large groups of young people who seem to be drinking more heavily than previously.

I do not look back with rose-tinted glasses, nor do I crave some sort of romantic ideal; that said the area of Surrey where I was brought up, with its small towns, large dormitory estates and picturesque villages contained pubs of all type and size. Some were frightful, one visit quite enough, but the majority had two bars, saloon and public, often with a snug/off sales area in between, and were places I enjoyed visiting by myself, with a mate, a girlfriend, a cricket team, whatever. On the whole locals made you welcome and nearly all of them had customers of all ages and types. Talking and drinking with people in these places was not just enjoyable, it was a constant source of learning, coming to accept different opinions and I made many friends over the years that, without a pub in common, may never have met. When I moved to London as a naïve 20 year old I found some of the big city pubs a little threatening but soon found my way round and enjoyed finding new and enjoyable places to visit.

Throughout this book there will be mention of different opening and licensing hours over the years: my own strong opinion is that while there has probably never been a golden age, the current 24 hour opening legislation, allied to the smoking ban (I am a non-smoker) has been an unmitigated disaster and should be repealed/adjusted as soon as is practicable.

The clock may not go back, but Belloc was and remains right.

# GOOD HONEST BEER

## A NOTE ON THE VALUE OF MONEY

In a story that covers a period of well over a century there are countless mentions of money. I have consulted various indices and, in order to give some idea of contemporary values, I include a small table based on the retail price index.

The reader will note a large fall in the value of sterling allowed for during the post war period. As well as using several indices, I returned to Roy Jenkins's biography of Churchill and reacquainted myself with his estimations of his subject's literary earnings during the 1920s and 1930s. It cannot be an exact science but I think and hope I have given a reasonably accurate picture.

£1.00 today approximates to:

1878  £45
1900  £55
1910  £56
1920  £22
1930  £44
1940  £35

Three examples:

The salaries awarded to the directors of M&B at the time of the founding of the company in 1898 approximated to £200,000 pa today.

In the 1920s, M&B had cash in hand to the value of £12,500,000 today.

At today's prices Sir William Waters Butler's total estate had a value of £17,500,000 at the time of his death in 1939.

# GOOD HONEST BEER

## PREFACE

Throughout the nineteenth century Birmingham, in common with the rest of the United Kingdom, expanded rapidly in population, size, industry and commerce. A city of 144,000 inhabitants in 1831 became, by 1871, occupied by 344,000 and a further 30 year expansion led to a population of 522,000 at the time of Victoria's death. An Irish population of around 5,000 in 1830 more than doubled over the next 30 years.

The 1871 census records Birmingham's population precisely as 343,787. People had left the land in droves and moved into the cities in search of the jobs generated by Britain's industrial supremacy. While our foreign trade at £547 million in 1870 dwarfed that of The United States' £165 million, the agricultural and farming industry was in a state of collapse. Following the end of The American Civil War in 1865, the rapid opening of the prairies led to far cheaper imported grain and the decade of the 1870s shows a decline of over 92,000 British agricultural jobs. By 1871 just 15% of the workforce were employed in agriculture while 44% worked in industry, manufacture and mining, mainly working and living in the larger cities of the country.

The gradual enfranchisement of working people from the time of the first reform bill in 1832 and its successors in 1867 and 1884 meant that new generations of working city people started to have a say in their day to day living and their health, housing, education and leisure time. The electoral reforms of 1867/8 led to important changes for the populations of the major cities: Birmingham, Leeds, Liverpool and Manchester all increased their MPs from two to three members (still incredibly modest representation) whilst all male house owners and various dwelling house occupiers became enfranchised, resulting in one in six ratio of men having the vote, the electorate rising from 2,618,453 in three years to 4,380,000. While it is sobering to reflect that women were not to be fully enfranchised until 1928, working urban populations could no longer be ignored by public servants at either local or national level. As Joseph Chamberlain noted:

'The working classes…are now the majority in most branch constituencies, and no candidate and no policy has a chance of success unless this good-will and active support can be secured'.

Accordingly, city politicians, councillors and public servants planned, built and rebuilt their cities, installing all manner of basic amenities such as sewerage and fuel systems alongside social institutions like concert halls, libraries, universities and schools with a passion and speed utterly out of step with such projects today. Essentially the overall aim was to enable people to live better, longer, healthier and, hence, more productive lives which would contribute to the overall well-being of the nation. Whilst laudable in intention, there was an element of people being subjected to middle class values whether they liked it or not.

This was to be especially true of the legislation and agitation against the drinks industry after 1850 when many middle class commentators were convinced that drunkenness was the sole cause of poverty and could not accept that many working class people turned to drink as an escape from their lousy living and working conditions. Later in the century as the parks, music halls and other social amenities became more numerous and accessible in the cities, it came to be recognized that people needed a chance to have a more rounded life.

# CHAPTER 1: THE BREWERIES & VICTORIAN LEGISLATION
## BIRMINGHAM'S BREWERIES IN THE 19<sup>TH</sup> CENTURY

Beer has been brewed and drunk in this country for over 1,500 years. The un-hopped drink of the fourth century probably had little to do with beer as we know it today, especially as one Roman Emperor suggested it made you smell of goat. There are mentions of brewing enterprises in the Domesday Book and brewing began at Burton 200 years later in 1295. Henry 11 imposed duty charges in 1188, while Henry 111's Assize of Ale continued in some form or other until 1780. While never ceasing to be amazed at the lengths to which chancellors will go to extract more duties, one really has to hand it to our Plantagenet ancestors: they charged duty on goods being shipped from Normandy to England despite owning both of them, tax being payable both on the export and the import. Even Brussels today would be hard pressed to better that.

While duty on drink itself is an important part of this story, it is more relevant to note the early laws passed relating to licensed premises, and in particular pubs. Henry V11 was keen to keep folk out of the pubs and practising their archery skills (in case he needed an army at short notice) and introduced licensing laws in 1495. Assorted legislation followed in 1552 and 1618 before the puritan rulers of Cromwell's government came down hard on all forms of 'pleasure'. The resultant Restoration in 1660 led to a liberal period where public drunkenness became almost a virility statement, again followed by a crackdown in 1753 when all licences became subject to annual renewal.

Following Britain's eventual triumph against Napoleonic France in 1815, government had to accept that society had dramatically changed. The population was growing fast, the countryside began to empty as the towns and cities filled and a vast expansion of industrial activity was taking place. The sheer speed of change is breathtaking to look back on: just, for a moment, consider the building of the railway system. Following the building of 150 miles of line in South

Wales before 1812, the Stockton and Darlington railway was commissioned in 1821, Birmingham was reached from London in 1838 and by 1850 there were nearly 5,000 miles of line in the kingdom. Even with considerable doubts expressed about the efficiency of steam locomotives, a vast network of passenger and freight movement was conceived, debated and constructed in 30 odd years. In 2010 we were looking at six years of planning before a high speed link from London even sees a spade.

With this rapid expansion came obvious social issues and government was especially concerned by the possible outbreak of unrest and political agitation, much of its ideology imported from Jacobin France. The feverish atmosphere of the 1820s, the desire for parliamentary reform and representation led to a wave of legislation, including the 1830 Beerhouse Act. It is worth considering this Act in some detail as it created the conditions by which many thousands of Victorians relaxed for the next half century and resulted in the massive expansion in licensed premises that eventually edged government towards some form of state control. As we shall see, M&B, and especially William Waters Butler, came to believe that a policy of 'fewer and better' pubs would both placate government and enable them to build up their businesses.

Proposals to change licensing laws would today be debated in some detail but they would be unlikely to lead to a change of government whereas in 1830 that possibility was very real. The Act was considered by many vested interests to be almost revolutionary while some historians today consider the Act as important as the first reform bill of 1832. Magistrates at this time controlled the licensing of all liquor outlets and there was widespread corruption with considerable sums of money changing hands to facilitate the granting of new licences. Sums as much as £1,000 changed hands in London as the brewers and courts were restricting trade to their own ends which led to a real and understandable agitation for free trade. There were modest attempts in 1823 and 1824 to free up the trade and by 1830 there had been a 7% increase in alehouse licences and a much larger

23% growth in spirit ones. As we see today, the pricing of alcohol and the relationship between beers, ciders and stronger drink was a matter for public debate. Beer prices were high in the period after 1815 whilst spirit duties were lowered, ostensibly to offset the smuggling trade, which led to an enormous increase in stronger drink consumption. In 1722 the average Briton consumed an average half a gallon of spirit each year and this had nearly doubled a century later leading to a national swallowing of 12 million gallons per annum by 1833. Tea and coffee were becoming more popular but it became palatable to consider a growth in beer sales to offset spirit ones.

The Duke of Wellington had become Prime Minister in 1827 and by 1830 his government was in considerable difficulty. The failing health of George 1V and his possible death would, constitutionally, lead to a general election, while Ireland and Corn Law legislation were both thorny problems and a 'popular' measure was seen as requisite: today we might call it an election giveaway.

It is noteworthy that that the Labour government in power from 1997 annually increased the duties on beer while leaving that on some spirits, especially whisky, alone. Is it mischievous to note that the chancellor was a Scottish MP? Certainly this policy led to a levelling in prices and the purchase of strong drink became vastly more affordable, a far cry from the 1970s when a tipple was twice the price of a pint.

The Duke himself had experienced at first hand the danger of a large body of drunken men, notably during the Peninsular War, and especially at the notorious sacking of Badajoz where he only regained control of his looting soldiers by erecting gallows in front of them. His government's primary proposal was to abolish the beer duty and to introduce a system whereby, in exchange for a two guinea licence, any person could legally brew and sell beer. The existing brewers were not impressed but the bill gradually worked its way through both Houses of Parliament despite the death of the King on the 26th June. The London brewers were reasonably relaxed about the measures as they considered their distribution and professionalism would protect market share, but their country cousins fought long and hard against the Bill which finally passed into law on the 12<sup>th</sup> July 1830.

Interestingly, in a recent biography of Wellington, I noted that this 1830 legislation was never mentioned which, given its importance, seems a little strange.

Duties on strong beer (at ten shillings per barrel) and cider were repealed and the two guinea scheme was earmarked for opening on the 11<sup>th</sup> October. The resulting beerhouses were to be allowed to open from 5 am until 10 pm (still shorter hours than the spirits trade) except Sundays. Within six months 24,324 new licences were purchased and granted but, despite an initial surge, beer consumption was actually to fall by 1850.

The 1830 Beerhouse Act emphatically did not harm the health of the nation and enabled many people of limited means to run a modest business. However, the proliferation of beer houses brought the whole brewing industry into the focus of magistrates and especially the forces of temperance. From the time of the Act there were numerous attempts to legislate the drinking habits of the people and for the next half a century there was an undeclared war between the temperance movement, organized religious groupings and genuinely driven individuals and the breweries, publicans and their customers.

There still remained the issue of the breweries and taxation. From earliest times, via our Plantagenet ancestors, rulers have seen the vast potential for raising revenues from the sale of alcohol. Victorian chancellors were no different, anxious to keep the books of UK Limited balanced, while watching their political backs.

From a national perspective, we now move to Birmingham itself. In 1817 there were four principal breweries in Birmingham, all situated either in or very close to the centre of the city. Richards & Co., formerly Richards & Goddington, were in Deritend. Down the road from the Bull Ring, Forrest & Son worked from Warstone Lane in the Jewellery Quarter, the Union Brewery traded off Broad Street, very close to William Butler's eventual site, and the Britannia Brewery resided at New Town Row. This last named was one of the biggest breweries in the UK outside of London but closed in 1819.

The vast growth in the cities of Victorian Britain heralded an explosion in licensed premises. In 1835 Birmingham housed 497 public houses which grew, by 1880, to 670 while the growth of beer houses, those not allowed to sell spirits, in the same 45 year period saw 423 houses become 1,514, giving the chancellor of the day a target of over 2,000 licensed premises in just the one city. Not only were banks willing to lend money to brewers, but these enterprises benefited from advances in steam and electrical power, and new technologies in the brewing of their principal product. Coke took over from wood as the principal fuel while the wooden brewing vessels were replaced by cast iron and copper ones. Manual labour was reduced by the introduction of cast iron mash tuns, and mechanized mashing itself became the norm. The whole brewing process was completely overhauled by temperature control which enabled brewers to produce more beer using less malt. Davenports opened in 1829 moving from their initial site at 120 Brearley Street to Bath Row in 1852. Joseph Ansell started his business as publican of The Hope & Anchor in Fisher Street in 1838 before moving to the junction of Lichfield Road and Park Road, Aston in 1857. The Belle Vue Brewery was opened in 1850 followed by the Union Brewery in 1851, Edward Cartwright's brewery at Snow Hill (1852), Mathew Bower's Albion Street Brewery at Ladywood (1854), Thomas Smith's Ashted Brewery (1859), both William Hollister's Handsworth Steam Brewery and James Bate's business at Kings Heath (1860) and Walker & Sons Birchfield Brewery in 1863. These fast-working Victorians seem to have stopped for a breather for a full seven years before Holder's Midland Brewery opened in Nova Scotia Street in 1870 to be quickly followed by John Dawber's Mazeppa Brewery, Aston (1875), Joseph Forrest's company in Winson Green Road (1877), and then in 1878 a further three breweries opened: Henry

# GOOD HONEST BEER

Fulford, Holt Street, Atkinson's Brewery, Queens Road, Aston and Birmingham Brewing, Malting and Distilling company. This last named company went into liquidation in 1882 as had the Albion Street Brewery six years earlier. This frenzied activity of opening/trading/takeovers all happened in the space of time a modern government seems to need to have one public inquiry. And neither Messrs. Butler nor Mitchell have yet been mentioned.

As a rough guide, in the second half of the 19th century incomes rose by 90% while, thanks to union negotiation, trade boards and general awareness of workers' rights, the hours of work reduced by 20%. Consequently people had more money and more time to spend on their leisure, and despite the disapproval of certain groupings, the drinks trade was the greatest winner.

Addressing The Royal Commission on Friendly Societies in 1871, it was suggested that the working man had become a 'respectable artisan: they go home at night and cultivate their gardens, or read the newspapers to their wives, instead of being in public houses'. While there was a determined effort to offer other leisure activities and a vast programme of garden allotments was devised to provide healthy exercise and good cheap food, this may certainly have been true of some, but it strikes as a massive exercise in self-delusion. Drinking undoubtedly was the main working class recreation.

Until 1869, following the 1830 Beer Act, a beer house could be opened on the back of a two guinea licence. There were occasional attempts to legislate against the social consequences of drunken behavior: Saturday night closing at midnight until noon on Sunday was introduced in London in 1839. Drunkenness was a problem and the courts were continually processing cases of 'drunken and disorderly' which by the 1870s were stabilizing but a running sore nevertheless. There was a period in the early 1870s when the city suffered an outbreak of gang warfare. In addition there was always the problem of a badly run house. In 1868 a Birmingham publican was fined £5 for 'unlawfully keeping his house…for the purpose of fighting cocks'. How much the fine deterred this errant gentleman can only be guessed at.

Of far greater consequence was the passing of legislation in 1869 that returned the issue of beer house licences to the control of local magistrates. Money alone was no longer sufficient for obtaining a licence; the courts clamped down on urban licences in particular in an effort to cut down on drunkenness. During the slum clearances in Birmingham during the 1870s, 57 licensed premises were demolished and most of these licences were not reissued. During the 1870s/1880s established brewers of good reputation recognized their opportunity to buy licences from magistrates, buy premises, supply them themselves and thus created the 'tied' house, an integral part of the M&B story. By 1892 The Brewer and Publican publication was not only commenting on this system as 'one of the chief aims of British breweries', but, even more importantly, noted that 'owners vie with one another in their efforts to make their houses look as attractive and stylish as possible'.

In principle everybody benefited; the legal authorities were content to see well-run houses, the brewers were happy and customers were treated to a better drinking experience than before. Equally the whole system of the tied house has been a concern for monopoly inquiries ever since. A Report on the Supply of Beer in 1969 from the Monopolies Commission and The Beer Orders of 1990, following the 1989 report and the policies subsequently followed by the 1997-2010 administrations played an important part in bringing the viability of some breweries down and contributed directly to the eventual demolition at Cape Hill.

During the early 1870s there was a profound political change in the relationship between the breweries and the establishment. Prior to 1871 the breweries were naturally inclined towards the Liberals. James Stansfield, a cabinet member of Gladstone's first premiership, was a brewer and largely sacrificed his career while campaigning against contagious diseases in the 1880s. The head of Bass sat as a

GOOD HONEST BEER

Liberal MP from 1848-83. The widening enfranchisement of voters in 1832, and more importantly in 1867, made it essential for political parties to extend their influence into the cities in search of the working man's vote.

By the mid-1870s drink consumption was booming and the beer slump of the 1850s was well and truly over. 1876 marked the zenith of beer production at an average annual national consumption of 34.4 gallons, or 275 pints. By 1900 and even more by 1914 these levels were falling fast but in the 1870s the state was incredibly exercised by 'drink'. Temperance societies such as The British Temperance League (formed 1835), The Band of Hope (1847), The United Kingdom Alliance (1853), The National Temperance League (1856) and the Church of England Total Abstinence Society (1862) campaigned for temperance legislation. The United Kingdom Alliance in particular badgered the Liberals and via a bill introduced by Sir Wilfred Lawson and backed by 800,000 signatures forced through the legislation repealing the 1830 Beer House Act. And all through this period there is constant tinkering with opening hours. Between 1828 and 1874 there were eleven separate pieces of legislation. In 1830 beer houses were allowed to open at Sunday lunchtime from Ipm-3pm. Tinkered with in 1834, 1840, 1848, 1854, 1855 and 1872, the 1874 Licensing Act decreed that henceforth beer houses were to be allowed to open from 1pm-3pm on Sunday lunchtimes. One feels pity for the poor clerks having to record the mountains of hot air expelled on this subject.

By 1874 the drinking lobby's vote had moved to perhaps its more natural home, the Tory Party, and Gladstone was to note after his defeat that year: 'we have been borne down in a torrent of gin and beer'.

## CHAPTER 2: BIRMINGHAM: THE INDUSTRIAL LANDSCAPE
## JOSEPH CHAMBERLAIN & MUNICIPAL REFORM

By the 1870s Birmingham was an industrial powerhouse. Making full use of the added capacity that steam-driven machinery gave to an enterprise, factories and workshops had sprung up all over the city. 10,000 people were employed in the brass industry alone and the city became renowned for its buttons, guns, jewellery, pens and pins.

By 1874 there were 28 gun barrel makers in the city, mainly concentrated in an area known as the Gun Quarter. Largely buried today under urban dual carriageway, the area between the Fazeley Canal, Bath Street and Price Street is still visible and we will be visiting the site of The Gunmakers Arms later. As well as the gun barrel makers, there were 301 other companies involved in the process of gun manufacture and well over half of these were located in this tight little area which enabled highly specialist craftsmen to flourish, each providing that special piece of knowledge that eventually turned out the completed firearm. The Jewellery Quarter followed this pattern and the area is still clearly identified on modern street maps.

Away from these specialist groupings there were many other vastly successful enterprises. Joseph Gillott had a steel pen factory, the Victoria Works in Graham Street, and increased his production twentyfold by the introduction of a steam driven process which enabled his company to produce more than 10,000,000 ink nibs each week.

Although never a magnet for specialist groupings, Smethwick quickly became home to a large network of factories and smaller business operations. And it is in Smethwick where a young Joseph Chamberlain made a considerable fortune before becoming a councillor in 1869.

GOOD HONEST BEER

Chamberlain was not a Birmingham man. Born in London in 1836, his father sent him up to the Midlands in 1854 to look after his investment and partnership in a screw making company, Nettlefolds and Chamberlain. Joseph Nettlefold had acquired a patent from an American businessman enabling him to make turning screws in Great Britain and had persuaded the young Joe's father to sink some capital into the concern. Joseph Chamberlain became involved in the finance and accounting of the business which flourished in its Smethwick factories. The Chamberlain partnership was dissolved in 1874, and became Nettlefolds Ltd. before, in 1902, becoming Guest Keen and Nettlefold. William Butler certainly benefited from this company as the works were situated around Heath Street, in a factory clearly marked on local maps as The London Works, and a proportion of the workforce would have slaked their thirst in nearby London Street at The London Works Tavern. Later William Waters Butler was to acquire shares in the company and the author remembers receiving dividends from the company for many years.

Chamberlain was not the first man to advocate municipal reform but he introduced a new vitality into the whole process. His great success as a businessman persuaded him to introduce the economics of the marketplace into the public sector: vast borrowings financed his projects and, possibly to the irritation of his many opponents, produced healthy profits. His early contemporaries on the council were thus described: 'the personnel of the old town council was remarkable. The leading lights were very homely, old fashioned citizens who used to meet at the Old Woodman in Easy Row to arrange the business, so that at council meetings time was not lost'. He allied himself to three councillors, Messrs. Avery, Collings and Harris and together they formed a small party known as The Municipal Reformers. In 1870 this small grouping forced the main council to consider operating the terms of the Workshops Act (1867) primarily aimed at improving sanitary and educational standards.

Despite earlier attempts to legislate for improvement in city living conditions, like The Municipal Corporations Act of 1835, and a report from 1842 called 'The Sanitary conditions of the Labouring Classes', in 1845 only 8,000 Birmingham dwellings (from a stock of 40,000) had mains water. The Public Health Act of 1848 set up a central board of health which had powers to create local boards in areas where death rates from disease were unacceptably high, but this measure failed, largely because once the power had been divested locally, no central leverage was allowed. Sanitary inspectors were introduced on a national scale in 1866 and in 1871 a royal commission, started three years earlier, recommended strong measures 'necessary for civilized social life'. These included a sound water supply and drainage and for the first time looked at pollution caused by smoke and rotting rubbish.

In 1854 a Dr. Snow had shown that cholera spread virulently through water-borne sewage and many people considered beer to be safer than water. Eton College brewed its own beer until 1875 and beer was served with food at Winchester College until 1872. The Quakers themselves brewed beer until discovering the benefits of tea (with boiled water of course). Mixed attitudes to alcohol consumption continued: in 1851 The Great Exhibition (where Joseph Nettlefold acquired his patent) was an alcohol free zone, but as late as 1876 Disraeli was being prescribed port for his bronchitis, asthma and gout.

Back in Birmingham an injunction was taken out against the city corporation restraining its dumping of raw sewage in the River Tame. A study/report was presented to the council in June 1871 recommending the purchase of over 2,000 acres of land for sewage clearance and an expenditure of some £275,000 suggested for its implementation as a working station. In practice fine, but councillors, including Chamberlain, objected on the grounds that the 'estimates were vague, the lands unsuitable, the works underestimated, and the beneficial results problematical'.

Chamberlain further explained his objection on the basis that clean water supply was 'not a legitimate source of profit' and 'it seems to me absolutely certain that…the power of life and death should not be in the hands of a commercial company, but should be conducted by the representatives of the people'.

A new Sewage Inquiry Committee was formed and its report led the way to the formation of a thoroughly efficient sewage department. Moreover Chamberlain's membership of this committee (he did not attend one of its 19 meetings) led directly to his nomination for mayorship.

As a municipal reformer, Chamberlain is primarily noted for the acquisition of safe water, gas supplies and a massive programme of slum clearance. The main water supply to the city from the rivers Elan and Claerwen in Wales is still his legacy. But he also played a leading role in encouraging the growth of new parks and the paving of footpaths. And he concerned himself with the 'drink problem'.

In 1870 Birmingham was actually one of the more sober cities in England. Perhaps as a result of good levels of employment and the absence of port traffic, there were 2,244 cases of drunkeness recorded in the city that year compared to 11,083 in Manchester and 21,113 in Liverpool.

Chamberlain's municipal work brought him into contact with the police force of Birmingham and at monthly meetings he became aware of the concern expressed at the levels of drunkenness. In 1877, after he had been elected as a Liberal MP, he brought forward his own plan for public-house reform. After careful study he proposed the adoption of a system based in Sweden called the Gothenburg system which called for all the profits from an alcoholic drinks outlet to be reinvested in the community it served. Birmingham Council seemed minded to accept this far-reaching proposal but despite winning plaudits for his speech moving his resolution on the 13th March 1877, the measure itself was powerfully rejected in the House of Commons.

With increased voting rights, the working classes became more vociferous in demanding a basic education for all. In 1867 the

Birmingham Education Society was formed and Chamberlain stood on its committee. This new grouping comprehensively surveyed the city and found that less than 40% of children of school age were actually in education. Although a marked increase over results obtained in 1838 and, with the enormous increase in population an achievement of sorts, the committee was not satisfied. In 1869 they formed the National Education League with a view that every child in the land would receive proper schooling. Opposed by vested church interests and competing with other municipal committees like the Manchester based National Education Union, this grouping was largely responsible for the resulting Forster Education Act of 1870. (Interestingly, it seems that W E Forster and Chamberlain thoroughly disliked each other but were prepared to work together for the common aim.) Local school boards were set up to ensure that all children within their districts were found a school place and treasury grants with local rate supplements were provided to facilitate these first moves into a national comprehensive form of education. We will see later how much education mattered to William Waters Butler. Born in 1866, the son of a publican, he would be a beneficiary of this legislation and he was to be a champion of further education all his life.

The debates, political intrigues and parliamentary process surrounding the 1870 legislation were the first proper exposure Chamberlain experienced at national level and it was inevitable that he would eventually move onto a bigger stage. Chamberlain left municipal affairs after accepting the post of President of the Board of Trade in 1880 but his mayorship made a huge impact on Birmingham and created so many of those better conditions that were to aid entrepreneurs such as Henry Mitchell and William Butler.

It is wrong to suggest that living conditions for the working class people of Birmingham were ideal by the late 1870s. Both work and domestic arrangements were often cramped, smelly and, to some extent, dangerous. But the lot of the working person was steadily improving. The extension of the franchise had forced the hand of government at both local and national level and the city dweller now had a say in how he worked and how he played. Any person looking to open a business in what is now called the 'leisure industry' could not afford to ignore this growing market.

In many ways 1870 is seen as a major social watershed in the history of this country. Following the upheaval from land to town, the rise in population, the incredible burst of inventive energy in all aspects of industry and domestic life, the limited emancipation of the working man, the increase in wages, the improvement in living conditions and the overall wealth of the nation, there could never be a return to the slower, more rural England. In the next hundred years this incredible rate of change would be maintained and, with the added trauma of world conflict, society would continue to progress along very different lines. Throughout this often turbulent era, attitudes towards religion, marriage and all aspects of social behavior would in turn be examined and debated in detail and throughout this period men and women would continue to drink alcohol either at home, at social gatherings or in the 'pub'. In some ways the 'pub' was to be the one real constant for over a hundred years. It is arguable that until the 1990s the local inn, whether on a village green or in an urban back street, remained a focal point for the community in which it stood. Certainly there would be new designs, new drinks and fashions, but the 'pub' was always there. Today that is rapidly changing and perhaps now is an opportune time to look back at one particular enterprise that in so many ways epitomized this constant.

M&B was to be a focal point for a community for over a century. They were to employ many thousands of men and women both directly in their breweries and pubs and, indirectly, in agriculture and transport. The taxes raised against their products would amount to very considerable sums for the treasury of the day and, despite the dangers inherent in their product, were surely a force for good in their time.

## CHAPTER 3: HENRY MITCHELL

Henry's father, also named Henry, was born in Bromyard, Worcestershire in 1810. He ran away, aged 14, to become an apprentice with a company of glove makers, Dents. He then became a builder before marrying Sarah who died a young woman. Henry then moved onto Stourbridge, where it is believed he met his second wife, Ruth. Another move followed, to Dudley, before he became a publican for the first time in 1851 at the age of 41. His first pub was The Oddfellows Arms in Hall Street, West Bromwich and he quickly moved on to the Cape Inn on Spur Lane next to the Birmingham Canal. Eight boats passed his pub daily as part of the packet service; drawn along by horsepower, this opened the opportunity to offer livery as well as refreshment. The use of sites near to toll roads and canals will be seen as a recurring theme in the early story of the founders of M&B. An advertisement hanging from the inn wall proclaimed:

'Well Air'd Beds – Good Stabling – Excellent Wharfage'

Always restless, Henry moved yet again in 1854 to The Crown Inn, Oldbury Road, Smethwick. The modern visitor can still see how close he was to the Birmingham Canal and the turnpike road from Birmingham to Dudley. Henry was now content, brewing enough beer to make his pub self-sufficient and he settled into running a successful business.

By 1861 Henry, aged only 51 and ready to retire, had a ready-made successor. Born on the 3$^{rd}$ November 1837, Henry Mitchell, eventual co-founder of M&B, was, at the age of 24, eager to take on and expand his father's business. The Crown was valued at £510.10s and consisted of 'kitchen, jack crane & meat jack, tap room, bar or liquor shop, malt room, two attics, club room at the front of the house, sign, longwater trough, lamp, four cellars'. Current values suggest that the business was worth in excess of a quarter of a million pounds. Henry Mitchell (senior) retired to a house on St Paul's Road.

Henry was keenly interested in the technical side of the brewing business and, while retaining existing brews, he set about producing new products such as his 'Light Mild Ale'. Henry quickly saw the potential for selling his products to other innkeepers which would in turn lead to the future development of a tied house estate. In 1866 Henry built The Crown Brewery on land adjoining the inn. Starting at midnight on Sundays, 14 brews a week soon became the norm until work ceased at 10pm on Saturdays. By 1871, 12 men were employed, including Joseph Parker who had also worked for Henry's father and doubled as both an ostler and as a brewer. How much he ran the brewery side is not known, but he undoubtedly brought a wealth of experience and good practice to Henry's enterprise. Even at this early stage, Henry faced stiff competition: John Jordan and Henry Jerams were brewing in Oldbury itself, while Walter Showell and Samuel Woodhall operated in Langley and West Bromwich respectively. Full capacity was soon reached and, despite having additional maltings both locally in Smethwick and also West Bromwich and Birmingham itself, by the mid-1870s Henry was actively looking for land on which to build a completely new brewery. Across the borough where today Grove Lane meets Cape Hill and Dudley Road, he found and purchased initially seven, later 14, acres of land, part of Fawdry's Farm. The year was 1878. The farm straddled the junction of the city boundary and Cape Hill was erected, as shown on the 1901 Ordnance Survey, in Staffordshire, thus giving weight to the argument that M&B was never, strictly speaking, a Birmingham brewery. On the 21st of March he laid the first brick of his new brewery. Designed by the London-based architects, Scamell & Colyer, and still named The Crown Brewery the first brew was ready in July 1879. This building was later to be known as No 1 Brewery.

Henry moved his wife Anne and their four children, Henry, Edward, Laura and Herbert, from Paxton House, South Road to Kelvin Grove, one of three large properties that aligned the Cape Hill site. Henry eventually was to live in Augustus Road, Edgbaston just a few hundred yards from William Waters Butler's house in Norfolk Road

Henry Mitchell and William Butler The portrait of Butler was found by the author hanging in The London Works Tavern, Smethwick.

The Crown, Broad Street: site of William Butler's brewery.

The author outside The London Works Tavern William Butler was the licensee 1866-1875. William Waters Butler was born here.

William Waters Butler and his great-grandson

Southfield: a view from the rear in 2009.

The Orangery at Southfield where William Waters Butler kept his collection of orchids

# GOOD HONEST BEER

Cape Hill Brewery as designed for Henry Mitchell in 1878 and (below) how it looked by 1929. In the lower picture, the War Memorial can clearly be seen standing outside the main offices. Today it stands in front of the Fire Station, the first major building past the trees on the front left of the picture.

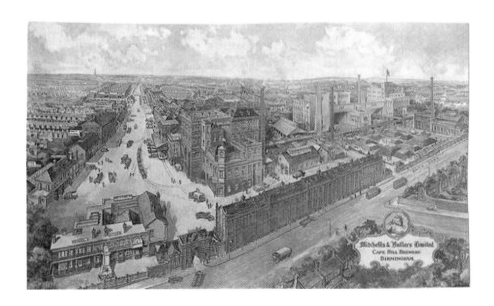

Armistice Sunday 2010 The M&B Fire Station stands behind the gathering.

Vernon Fisher demonstrates the original site of the memorial: compare to the picture on Page 37.

Two views of the memorial today. The author and Vernon Fisher

A very heavy Ambulance Division Cup and, lest we forget, what it was all about…

(where we will visit later). Henry was obviously intrigued by property and in 1895 he bought Elmhurst Hall, a 640-acre estate situated north of Lichfield. It seems he let the estate, but after his death his executors failed to find buyers which led to its demolition in 1921.

By 1881 both mild and pale ales were being brewed as well as a special 'Standard Shilling Family Ale'. Success followed success and in 1886 Henry turned his Henry Mitchell & Co into a limited company. His 14 acres of land now had assets of £585,602, employed 271 persons and brewed 90,000 barrels per annum, each containing 36 gallons, giving the local populace a chance to wade through 25,920,000 pints.

As part of further expansion Henry went into partnership (in 1888) with Mr. Herbert G Bainbridge whose family remained connected to M&B for over 50 years.

In 1888 a report reviewing the industrial power of Birmingham at the time reported thus on Henry Mitchell & Co. It is worth quoting at length as it gives an excellent contemporary view of Henry's reputation and of his enterprises. (Some older spellings have been changed.)

---

A review of the great industries which form the wealth and fame of Birmingham would be incomplete without detailed mention of the brewing trade, for this line is of considerable importance and influence owing to the wealth it represents, the number of hands it employs, and for its unsurpassable state of perfection. One of the most important firms established within recent years, and one that has gained a high reputation throughout the United Kingdom for the excellence and reliability of its brews, is that of Messrs. Henry Mitchell & Co., Cape Hill. This house was founded in 1866, twenty-two years ago, and from the first its sole aim has been to produce ales, etc., whose leading characteristics should be purity, strength, nourishing and appetizing qualities and general excellence.

# GOOD HONEST BEER

That it has been eminently successful is seen from the fact that the productions have received the commendation of the highest medical authorities, and throughout the country has been developed a great trade, which is increasing in a most gratifying manner. The business was originally established in the Oldbury Road, Smethwick but nine years ago the trade had become so heavy and was increasing so rapidly that the firm conceived the idea of erecting new premises.

The Cape Hill site was selected after due consideration, and the present spacious and lofty blocks of buildings were erected from specially advanced designs. The entire premises cover an area of nearly seven acres, and they comprise breweries, maltings wine and spirit and cigar departments, offices and stabling. Besides these premises it must be mentioned that the firm has very commodious and admirably arranged maltings at Winson Green, King Edward's Road and Broad Street, styled respectively Wellington Crescent and St. Peter's Maltings.

The breweries form a considerable portion of the Cape Hill premises, and they are excellently arranged and fully provided with all the latest improved machinery and appliances for the many operations carried on, which it is needless to remark are conducted on the most advanced principles. The total plant of this firm is of great value, and is acknowledged to be the largest and finest in the Midlands (excepting Burton), and the establishment in organization, equipment and supervision possesses exceptional facilities for the producing of the best ales. Messrs. Henry Mitchell & Co. also trade in wines, spirits and cigars, and the department devoted to these goods is admirably arranged and heavily stocked with the choicest wines, spirits of world-famous distillations, and cigars of the most noted brands. Great attention is paid to this department, and it is attended by the utmost success.

The stables, in which sixty and more horses are lodged, many of which are animals of great value, are models of cleanliness, well ventilated and warmed, and there is proper and suitable accommodation for stores, vehicles, and other paraphernalia appertaining to this department. In this extensive department a large number of skilled hands is employed, and the supervision in every department is all that could be desired. Messrs. Henry Mitchell & Co. brew on a very comprehensive scale, and their productions, including standard family ales, mild and pale ales, porter, stout and double stout, all of which, as above intimated, are brewed on advanced principles from the choicest English hops, and celebrated for their purity, nourishing, and appetizing properties and general excellence.

The trade built up by this firm upon these merits is of great magnitude and of the highest class, and which characteristic enterprise stories and agencies have opened in nearly every large town of the Unite Kingdom. Messrs. Henry Mitchell & Co. takes the liveliest interest in the welfare of their hands, and between employers and employees the most friendly relations exist. This is seen in the several recreational institutions formed by, and under the patronage of the members of the firm, and of which may be mentioned the Cricket Club and 'Mitchell's St. George's Football Club.'

These clubs hold the highest rank in the athletic world, and the Cricket Club, among their many successes, won the Birmingham District Challenge Cup of last year, whilst the record of the Football Club "is second to none" in the country. Another notable feature of this house is the Volunteer Fire Brigade, formed of the workplace under the captaincy of Mr. Henry Mitchell, junior, one of the respected members of this eminent firm. The Brigade does not confine its operations to outbreaks on the premises, for on many occasions under this gentleman's superintendence it has rendered valuable assistance in the neighbourhood. The members who constitute the firm are thoroughly conversant in every branch of the business, having had long and varied experience therein.

By their sterling qualities, and genial and courteous bearing they have won the esteem and confidence of the entire industrial and commercial world as well as the general community; and this house ranks among those great concerns that are universally acknowledged as the principal representatives of this famous national industry and trade.

---

Although somewhat flowery and repetitive, the emphasis on investment and medical excellence shows us how determined Henry was to be a market leader. In 1889 Henry jnr., known to his family as Harry, was dispatched to Paris to attend a beer festival where he collected a gold medal for the fine quality of Mitchell's ales and stouts and also, in his role as superintendent of Cape Hill's renowned fire brigade, won a silver medal for the company's brigade. We will visit the Fire Brigade in a later chapter.

Another report of the time, written by C. Meymott Tidy, M. B., and Barrister-at-Law, also Professor of Chemistry and Forensic Medicine at the London Hospital, Medical Officer of Health for Islington and an Official Analyst of the Home Office, followed a request by Henry to have his brewery and beers evaluated scientifically. After praising the buildings, the quality of the water drawn from the artesian wells below Cape Hill ('of remarkable organic purity and excellence') and the materials used for brewing, this estimable public servant selected five ales from stock and reported that 'after careful examination, that all the samples collected by me, both at and outside the works, were Beers of excellent quality, and free from any deleterious substances whatever'.

Despite all this success, it must never be assumed that running this vast business was anything but challenging. Both Henry Mitchell and, later, his partner, William Butler, would be exercised by government reports and legislation. The building of their tied house estates would, on the one hand, give them strength to develop their company but, on the other, would draw criticism from those who saw monopoly as undesirable, and especially those forces in society morally opposed to the liquor trade generally. In the 1880s the buying of estate and freehold properties was seen as progressive. In 1887/8 Henry Mitchell

& Co. Ltd. spent £60,000 purchasing licensed property, thus committing their entire gross profit for that year. At the following year's shareholders' meeting Henry said 'owing to the purchase of houses by other firms, the increasing competition and the falling off in the consumption of beer generally' that the company's business activity was diminished, a position only rectified by the purchase of a further 70 pubs. This policy was correct and a net profit of £22,000 was reported in 1888. By 1890 it had grown to £38,000.

Henry, like several of his contemporaries, believed in this building up of estates. Equally he was totally determined to supply his own pubs. After amalgamation with William Butler, he reported to the 1900 AGM thus:

When I commenced in the brewing trade, something like forty years ago, Birmingham was very differently supplied with beers from what it is now. At that time vast sums of money were annually sent to such centres as Burton-on-Trent, Dublin, London, Leeds, Edinburgh and Glasgow and in addition a great many publicans in Birmingham brewed their own beer. They brewed it in very disadvantageous circumstances, for their premises were as a rule poor, unsanitary and quite unfit for brewing clean and wholesome beer…Now Birmingham and district has quite a dozen large and well-equipped breweries capable of turning out some of the best beers brewed in England. Instead of sending vast sums of money away for its beers, Birmingham is now practically carrying on the industry by itself covering all requirements of the city and neighbourhood…The brewers have demolished lots of tumble-down, insanitary and useless public houses and provided well-built and well-managed places wherein may be carried on a respectable and wholesome trade'.

Not only did Henry think he was running a splendid business (indeed he was), but he could and did delude himself that beer was the perfect recreational drink. At the 1907 AGM he absolved beer as a contributor to drunken behaviour:

GOOD HONEST BEER

'There is no intoxication in these light beers. To meet a drunken man in the street is as rare now as to meet a badger in a wood. Of course there is intoxication; from the days of Noah there always have been and until the end of the world there will always be men who on some occasions take too much. But these men at the present moment are not British workmen who drink honest British beer; they are shufflers, who as a matter of common notoriety do not care for beer but drink spirits'.

This was obviously nonsense and one could wonder what many shareholders who probably enjoyed a tipple of scotch supplied by Henry thought of this.

So, in a very short time, Henry Mitchell had created and grown a very large enterprise, all the time ensuring the quality of his product. It is evident that he was not content to rest on his laurels and just a few years later he was to go into partnership with a William Butler and to form a new company, Mitchells & Butlers.

What did William Butler offer Henry and whence had he come?

## CHAPTER 4: ROBERT & WILLIAM BUTLER

The author is indebted to Martin Mellor for much of the information about Robert Butler, grandfather to William Waters Butler. Martin is churchwarden at the Leicestershire village of Burbage and I contacted him in November 2009 after coming across details of a talk he gave to a local CAMRA (Campaign for Real Ale) group entitled A Butler from Burbage. Truly does ale have its uses.

Robert Butler was born in Hinckley on the 31$^{st}$ October 1807 and was christened at St. Mary's, Hinckley. In July 1834 he married Mary Ann Liggins at St. Catherine's, Burbage. Their son, William, was born on the 13$^{th}$ March 1843 some five years after his future partner, Henry Mitchell. Robert traded throughout his life as a worsted hose weaver, which suggests clothing ranging from footwear to heavy duty coats and mackintoshes. My own researches suggested that he chiefly made socks as he carried his stock into Coventry once a week for market and anything heavier would surely have crippled him. According to the 1871 census Robert and Mary lived at New Buildings, Hinckley. Robert outlived his wife and spent his final days living at 2 London Road, Hinckley, cared for by a domestic servant named Ann Bell. It is reasonable to suggest that his son William, by then a wealthy man, facilitated this arrangement. Robert died in March 1904 and his gravestone informs us that aged 97 he was the oldest inhabitant of Hinckley. The Hinckley Times of the 26$^{th}$ March 1904 recorded his passing and talks of an elderly eccentric gentleman to be seen walking around his locality in an old style chimney pot hat. The splendid gravestone at St. Catherine's also records the death of his son, William, in 1907.

As Henry Mitchell's father had done before, young William left the countryside for Birmingham, where he worked as a hairdresser's assistant in St Martin's Lane, Deritend. He appears to have lived in a house near Broad Street, which he shared with Thomas Beckett and Phoebe Sillitoe. To supplement his income he got a part time job as a barman at The Old Crown on Broad Street, a pub that attracted trade from the roads and canals and offered spacious stabling. On market days, and especially during the annual Onion Fair, drinkers would crowd the extensive staircase that lined the outside of the building, while inside there was a clubroom available for political and other meetings. While working at The Crown, William met his future wife, Mary Ewing from Dumbarton, who was the sister-in-law of the landlord, G. Owen. On the 19th February 1866, at the age of 23, and by then experienced in pub work, William married Mary at Carrs Lane Chapel. On the same day he took over as proprietor of The London Works Tavern on the junction of Grove Lane and London Street, Smethwick, a few hundred yards up the road from Cape Hill and just along the road from the current site of the M&B War Memorial.

Today this is a somewhat depressed area, earmarked for redevelopment with a new hospital planned. According to a notice posted on the 3rd January 2011, The London Works Tavern is due for demolition. I visited the pub in 2009 when it was still trading. The landlord thought I was interested in buying it as he had seen me taking photographs outside, but once I had explained my interest he showed me round. I found a portrait of William Butler hanging in the corridor on the way to the toilets and after explaining who this old gentleman was, and that my great-grandfather had been born in the building in 1866, I was introduced to some locals who seemed happy enough to talk about the pub and locality.

A glance at the 1901 Ordnance Survey Map of Smethwick shows a large network of industrial units and factories. A well run pub hosted by a congenial landlord must have been quite a magnet for thirsty workers making their way home at the end of a draining shift. William Butler was covering all his bases. It is not certain to what extent William was brewing at this stage but he was producing enough for his own pub and gained an excellent reputation for his beer. It may have been the lack of available space that led him to move back to Broad Street after 10 successful years in Smethwick.

GOOD HONEST BEER

With all the factories and workshops packed into the immediate area around London Street it must have been a thriving business. A little later, in 1901, in an area from the Grove Lane/Dudley Road junction, up past William's business and across to the Cornwall Engineering Works there are over 10 pubs marked including three in the vicinity of Mollett Street.

William and Mary returned to Broad Street and The Crown in 1876 and William bought a new lease on the premises in 1880, at a rental of £840 a year, a substantial city centre rate, indicating that William, like Henry Mitchell, was ready to expand his business interests. Just three years later he had the opportunity to buy the premises although his landlords insisted on an auction in order to realize the highest price. Obviously determined to win, William bought The Crown and also purchased some cottages on King Edwards Place (clearly shown on 1901 maps as running down one side of The Crown) which he had demolished to make way for his own brewery which would eventually produce 5,000 barrels a week. William, like his future partner, saw the opportunity for selling beers to other publicans and provided them with loans, which effectively tied them and guaranteed sales for his beer.

As well as running a very successful business, William Butler became involved in charitable work and helped several Friendly Societies. He was trustee for numerous Trade and Money Clubs, including The Order of Forresters, The Oddfellows and local trade societies of carpenters and joiners. As an appreciation for these services, he was selected to lay a Foundation Stone at the Forresters' Convalescent Home at Clent, Worcestershire. To top all this he added his own loan club, Butler's Permanent Society. It will be seen that this involvement in charitable causes made a deep impression on his son, William, who in turn was to raise, lend and give considerable sums to worthy causes.

Mary predeceased William, dying on the 29th November 1899. William passed away on the 24th August 1907 at his home Elmdon in

Selly Oak. He was buried next to his wife in a vault at the non-conformist cemetery at Key Hill, Hockley.

William's passing was noted in the press and his cortege was witnessed by a large crowd of people lining the streets. The Tenants and Managers of the Licensed Premises, together with representatives of M&B, got together and formed a committee with a view to honouring William's life. Chaired by Arthur Wade Edge it was decided to purchase a plot of land and to erect cottages for employees of M&B who otherwise might have difficulties at the end of their service. The William Butler Memorial Cottages at Quinton have only recently been sold off individually. Enoch Wood and William Henry Kendrick (whom we shall encounter again) prepared and supervised the building free of charge and 20 local firms contributed to the actual building and connection of services, again free of charge. Work completed, William Waters Butler laid the foundation stone into which was placed a bottle containing a memorial to his father. William and his brother Henry decided to finance the rates and taxes on these properties and, in memory of their brother Albert Edward who had died in September 1908 aged just 30, paid for the construction of two further cottages.

It should also be recorded that the Mitchell family were responsible for building houses in the area. In 1927 ten almshouses were built in Cooper's Lane in memory of Henry Mitchell. Originally a family affair, the board of M&B took over the choosing of suitable tenants, while the Mitchell family financed the building of a further six properties. In 1946 Arthur Mitchell was to give £5,000 for the building of Hill Crest, a home for poor inhabitants of Smethwick, situated close to Cooper's Lane on the junction of Little Moor Hill and South Road. This home received financial help from M&B for many years, an endowment of £95 being recorded in 1965. Harborne Cottages, as the almshouse development became known, is still a thriving community run under the auspices of The Harborne Parish Lands Charity.

# CHAPTER 5: CAPE HILL & THE BIRTH OF M&B

The story of Cape Hill continues until 2002, but for the purposes of this chapter I have not described anything beyond 1939-45.

As we have seen, by the mid-1890s both Henry Mitchell and William Butler were running very considerable businesses with substantial estates of tied houses. By then the amount of beer brewed 'on site' as opposed to at a properly equipped brewery had diminished dramatically and it became harder and harder for one man bands to obtain licences. The courts and authorities were determined that, having got the cat in their bag, it would not escape again.

Brewers had to make a decision; either they stayed as they were and ran the risk of losing licences as they came up for renewal, thus losing market share, or they invested money in buying and leasing properties of good pedigree and acceptable to the authorities. In 1886 Arthur Guinness had become the first brewer to float in the city to raise capital in order to finance property purchase and expansion. The property explosion that followed led to higher prices, a bubble we still see today, followed by the inevitable crash.

However, properly financed and properly run, Henry Mitchell and William Butler saw this as the correct way forward and, with the land at Cape Hill still available for expansion, a merger between them had to make sense. A joint operation would give them greater power and perhaps protect them from any predatory takeover. How long initial negotiations took remains unknown: on the Butler side at least it seems that William's son was the driving force. An Extraordinary General Meeting of the shareholders of Henry Mitchell & Co. Ltd. was held at The Grand Hotel, Colmore Row on the 19th April 1898 to discuss the resolution that the Articles of Association were to

' be altered in manner following:-

That the name of the Company be changed to "Mitchells and Butlers Limited".

If approved this resolution would be submitted for confirmation at a further EGM to be held at the same venue on the 5th May.

Six Managing Directors were to be appointed each for an initial five year term: Henry Mitchell, John Edwin Mitchell, Arthur Mitchell, William Butler, William Waters Butler and Henry Alexander Butler. They were each to receive £4,000 a year basic salary, could earn bonuses, but 'the total sum to be paid to Managing Directors shall not, at any time, exceed the sum of £6,000 a year'. In other words, they were to be paid very well but not at a cost to the company that it could not afford, and monies were to be reinvested in future growth.

The success of this merger was staggering. Henry was a spare, thin man who seems to have been very conscious of keeping everything at Cape Hill strictly audited and under control, while William was more the party animal, cheery, full of bonhomie and very popular with his customers, a trick he had obviously learnt from his days running pubs. They may have been very different men but both were totally dedicated to the common aim: to brew the best beer possible, to provide better and better pubs in which to sample it and, in the process, make money. In just two years, Henry Mitchell's land bank of 14 acres had multiplied to 60 and by the outbreak of war in 1914 over 1,000 people were employed on the 90 acre Cape Hill site. During this initial 16 year period, three Birmingham competitors/breweries were acquired: The Vulcan Brewery of A. Homer Ltd. at Aston, with 56 tied houses and a capital valuation of £200,000, was taken over in 1899. Just one year later, J. Evans of Perry Barr was acquired and Smethwick's own Cheshire's Windmill Brewery became part of the new colossus in 1913. This Windmill Brewery stood at the junction of Raglan Road and Windmill Lane, barely a mile from Cape Hill. When the brewery was closed at the end of 1914, a letter was written to all existing customers stating that 'we purpose closing the Windmill Brewery…(which suggests somebody's spelling needed checking) and went on in a slightly bullying fashion:

'In place of these (beers and stouts) we can well recommend the qualities on enclosed list, brewed here. We do not sell Beers at 10d, ½, or 1/8 gallon. The only one quality of Strong Ale we have is XXXX, at 2/- per gallon as quoted'. There was certainly an element of take it or leave it.

It was not only through acquisitions and takeovers that the new company thrived. It was recognized that 'fewer and better' was desirable to the authorities and actually easier to run. In 1896 Arthur Chamberlain (brother of Joseph) was chairman of the Licensing Committee which held meetings with the Midlands Counties Wholesale Brewers Association with the express view of reducing the number of licensed premises and The Birmingham Property Company, formed in 1897 by local brewers, used a compensation scheme to facilitate the surrender of licences on run-down properties. Initially run as a voluntary operation, national licensing legislation passed in 1904 formalized these arrangements and M&B surrendered some 300 licences. We will see later that the building expansion of the 1920s and 1930s instigated by William Waters Butler and carried out in part by his son, Owen, owed much to the philosophy of the pre-war board and carried on the tradition that:

'Mitchells & Butlers houses contain clean airy rooms and more than a passing thought for the customer's well-being'.

At the time of Henry Mitchell's death in 1914, M&B was in a very strong position. In the financial year immediately preceding the Great War net assets had grown to £2,300,000 and a gross profit of £414,000 had been achieved. The company was well placed to deal with the considerable problems that the war itself and the legislation passed in those four years would pose.

GOOD HONEST BEER

## THE LAYOUT OF THE BREWERY

The modern visitor to Smethwick and Cape Hill can no longer take in the size of the brewery and the extent to which it dominated its immediate neighbours. If you start at the junction of Bearwood Road and Waterloo Road, walk down Waterloo road to a small roundabout, move forward to the crossroads where Windmill Lane goes left and Shireland Road right: you are now at the top of Cape Hill. On both sides of the road there are many small shops and businesses, often reflecting the multi-ethnic make-up of the borough today, and there is a modern retail development on your right. Pause at the entrance to Montague Road on your right and look down to the roundabout at the bottom of the hill where Cape Hill ends and Grove Lane and Dudley Road meet. That entire length of road constitutes the northern boundary of the brewery. At the bottom of the hill after passing along the new housing development built by Persimmon, there is a small turning right actually off the roundabout where you will find the War Memorial with the Fire Station on your left and you are at the far end of the brewery. Walk through the housing development, always working through in a straight line from the Memorial and you will see, by a row of trees, an old red brick building. This is the Pumping Station, which stood at the southern end of the cricket ground, the latter having disappeared under a mountain of soil excavated by the developers. You are now at the southern end of the brewery and close to where the railway sidings left the brewery for the short trip to Rotten Park Road Station and the connection back to the main line from Wolverhampton to Birmingham. Access to the western side is not too easy and a short walk back up Cape Hill to the junction with Montague Road is probably easiest. The brewery boundary extended along this road and you are standing on what was the bowling green, tennis court and other leisure facilities as well as the rear of No 2 brewery.

At the back of this book there is a map of the brewery drawn from a 1931 survey of the storm/rain drains throughout the site. A vast map, originally drawn in a scale of 30 feet to an inch, this has been reduced some 80 fold. The detail is not precise but the key below highlights some prime locations. Cape Hill itself is on the right of the map, the northern boundary.

A) No 1 Brewery: the original brewery built by Henry Mitchell
B) No 2 Brewery
1) General offices, boardroom etc
2) Fire Station: still standing in 2011, used by Persimmon as a showroom and site office. Some M&B memorabilia and the William Savage shield are displayed in a small ante room inside.
3A) The War Memorial, dedicated in 1922
3B) The War Memorial, rededicated in 2006
4) Stabling
5) Garage
6) Cricket Ground
7) Bottlery
8) Timber Stacking Yard
9) Cooperage (brand new in 1931)
10) Cask Stacking Yard
11) Cask Washing Shed
12) Kelvin Villa/Grove: Henry Mitchell lived here for a while. Later converted to flats for employees and their families.
13) Sports area: bowls and tennis
14) Pumping Station. Still standing in 2011 the railway into No 2 Brewery entered the site here.
15) The original entrance of the railway into No1. The railway bed is marked to its right. (See railway map on Page 72)

GOOD HONEST BEER

## WORLD WAR AND THE MEMORIAL

By 1914 the two original founders had died. William passed away in 1907 and Henry died, aged 76, at his home, the Cedars, 4 Augustus Road. Before his death he had seen the building and early operating of No 2 Brewery.

At the outbreak of war in August 1914, M&B, like many other concerns, had to contend with losing much of their male workforce to the war effort. At home, the war was to be a challenging time for the brewers. The government, and especially Lloyd George, became determined to reduce the amount of beer available and to limit the time in which it could be legally consumed. In a later chapter, The Carlisle Experiment, we shall see how this policy worked, the involvement of William Waters Butler, and its lasting effects.

At the turn of the century The Boer War had been a sharp wake up call for the British army. Eventually victorious, tactics had been shown to be outdated and a major review of the service was undertaken by Haldane, Secretary of state for War in the Liberal Government of Campbell-Bannerman. He visited Germany in 1906, watched its armies in field training, consulted his French counterparts and set in train a major reform of the army in 1908. Central to this reform was the formation of a Territorial Force, the forerunner of the current T.A. The volunteer forces, which had performed surprisingly well in South Africa, formed the backbone of this new force and the patriarchal nature of these units pervaded from the start. Encouraged by government, industry in particular led the way in the formation of new companies. While patriotism played its part there was the issue of physical fitness of the workforces: in Birmingham, Cadbury had become so worried by the lack of fitness in its young men that compulsory physical exercise had been introduced.

On the 17th January 1908, the Birmingham Daily Mail reported that '...Mitchells and Butlers ... sought to form an infantry unit as an initiation of the co-operative movement between employers and the Volunteer Force'.

The M&B Company became part of the 5th Royal Warwicks which was to serve with distinction in the war ahead. Following the outbreak of war, this company was immediately mobilized. On the 4th August M&B assured the men that their jobs were secure and that the company would top up their army pay to meet their peacetime wage packet.

The 5th became part of the 143rd (Warwickshire) Brigade and was to serve in France until the autumn of 1917. It is not the role of this book to tell their story. I have been lucky enough to have read Peter Caddick-Adams history of the 143rd (see bibliography) and I am indebted to The Royal Regiment of Fusiliers (Warwickshire) and, in particular, David Baynham, who helped me access details of some of the M&B personnel who went to war. I visited their museum in June 2011.

My grandfather, William Owen Butler, joined the battalion as a 2nd Lieutenant in September 1915. Examining his war office file, he seems to have suffered a certain amount of ill health (some a little embarrassing), and missed the carnage on The Somme in which the 5th were actively involved. Owen went into the front line in the Mericourt sector on the 18th October 1917.

After the Italian army had been soundly defeated at Caporetto in late 1917, 1918 found the 5th/6th/7th Royal Warwicks in Northern Italy as part of 48th Division, which along with 23rd Division garrisoned and patrolled an area of the front line facing Austro-Hungarian forces in the area of Asiago. On the 15th June, with the 5th in the front line, the Austrians went on the offensive, desperate to finally finish off the Italian war effort. The 5th soon found itself in dire trouble and were rescued in no small part by one man, Sergeant-Major Frank Townley, employed by M&B as chief travelling salesman. Already the holder of a Military Cross from an action at Ovilliers on the Somme,

Townley rounded up 13 cooks, clerks and backroom staff who proceeded to hold their position for six hours and were responsible for killing 91 enemy soldiers. For his part in this action, Townley was awarded a DCM. His citation in The London Gazette of 30<sup>th</sup> October 1918 reads:

'For conspicuous gallantry and devotion to duty during an enemy attack He gathered battalion headquarters together and covered all approaches to headquarters. He assumed command, and held off repeated efforts of the enemy to advance. His splendid example of cool fearlessness encouraged his men to hold the position until reinforced'.

This last major Austrian effort was repulsed over two days and the 5<sup>th</sup> garrisoned the area until the end of hostilities.

Whether Owen was involved in this action is not recorded but he was wounded on the night of 8th August while taking part in a raid on enemy trenches which netted 24 prisoners. Two Warwickshire personnel were killed on this raid, including Capt. H P Williams-Freeman, and a further 12 were wounded. Owen was sent home to recuperate and left the army in 1919, although he served in England with the 5<sup>th</sup> briefly in 1921 as a lieutenant.

Frank Townley continued to serve as a Territorial until 1938, when he received a MBE. His death in February 1948 was widely recorded. During the 1939-45 war he served as a Captain in the Cape Hill Brewery Company of the Home Guard, "D" Company, 31<sup>st</sup> South Staffs.

Owen Butler and Frank Townley were just two out of 1,359 persons from M&B who went to war, of whom 25 were decorated and 131 died on active service. Many of these men served in regiments other than the Royal Warwicks.

GOOD HONEST BEER

The company decided to erect a memorial in their memory and on the 1st October 1922 the memorial was unveiled and dedicated before a crowd of some 15,000 people. A Guard of Honour was commanded by William Owen Butler and his future wife, referred to as Miss Byrne, (Boo to me and my fellow grandchildren) was in attendance. The Guard of Honour comprised 63 men, including Frank Townley and several other recipients of awards for gallantry. As some of these men do not appear on the M&B Roll of Honour, I cannot confirm that every one of them worked for M&B at the time of their service, but it seems likely that all had some very good reason for being chosen for this duty.

The Guard of Honour is pictured on Page 68. Thomas Conniff (front row, second from the right) served as a machine gunner with the East Yorkshire Regiment, becoming a corporal. He is listed in the London Gazette of the 17th June 1919 as a Smethwick man and the recipient of the Military Medal.

Harry George McCabe served with the Coldstream Guards becoming a NCO. He too was awarded the Military Medal and appears in the Gazette in January 1918. Judging by his eventual discharge following a gunshot wound to the neck he was fortunate to survive. Other McCabes served who were employees of M&B; Harry does not appear to have been one but was a Smethwick man.

Samuel Plevey joined the Army Service Corps. This transport division attained Royal recognition in 1915. Samuel was another recipient of the Military Medal, gazetted in July 1918.

The Smethwick Telephone covered the event in their issue of Friday the 6th October 1922.

'----the memorial at Cape Hill was unveiled by Major-General Sir Richard Hoskins of the North Staffordshire Regiment. It was one of the most significant and impressive services possible to conceive. Over 15,000 people had assembled to pay homage to the 'glorious dead' and during the memorable scenes there was a solemn silence that was most inspiring. For some months past the completion of the memorial to the honoured memory from the firm of Mitchells & Butlers who fell in the Great War has been the object of the greatest interest to the thousands who cross the City boundary at Cape Hill'.

The article continued:

'---an address was delivered by Mr. W. Waters Butler, Chairman of Directors…the speaker then went on to recall that long before the outbreak of the Great War, the firm was approached by the officers of the Warwickshire Territorials to assist in the promotion of a Brewers Company'.

William went on to praise these men, some of whom had been a small part of our 'contemptible' army before stating that when victory finally came

'we cheered and we celebrated and perhaps for a moment we forgot at what cost we had attained that victory'.

Further names were added to the Memorial from both World War 2 and The Korean War. In 1942, on the 27th March, Able Seaman William Savage, employed by M&B in the sample cellar, was posthumously awarded the Victoria Cross 'for his courage while acting as gunner on the M.G.B. which was Commander Ryder's HQ in the raid on St. Nazaire Harbour, France...Able Seaman Savage worked the forward gun completely exposed to enemy fire until killed by an enemy shell at the end of the action'.

The Fire Station, happily now a listed building, contains a wooden plaque listing winners of The William Savage Memorial Medal, awarded by fellow members of the company to one or more people who, in the eyes of their colleagues, had performed or achieved something a little bit special in the course of a year.

In passing, there are also a couple of glass cabinets displaying some M&B memorabilia, including a few rather refreshing looking bottled ales. I am lucky enough to have a bottle of The Centenary Ale which is not for opening.

The War Memorial (see map) was sited just outside the brewery on Cape Hill. The picture on Page 38 shows Vernon Fisher demonstrating where the memorial originally stood. (The gentleman on his right is wondering whether The Angel of the North has just landed?) Following redevelopment of the area, the Memorial was re-sited outside the Fire Station where it was rededicated at a service held on Sunday the 1$^{st}$ October 2006. There was some concern locally that Persimmon, the developer, would not look after the Memorial. In fact they stored it and moved it to its current site. I visited the Memorial in 2009 with Vernon and a young friend, Emma Molland. I was then asked to attend the Armistice Service on the 14$^{th}$ November 2010 and to say a few words. This was a memorable occasion when I met many other M&B people and I had no hesitation in quoting William's words from 1922 as highlighted above.

On a summer visit to Cape Hill in 2011 I was pleased to learn that Persimmon will continue to support this annual gathering and I look forward to attending for many years to come.

GOOD HONEST BEER

THE FIRE BRIGADE

On my first visit to the War Memorial, in its new situation, I was intrigued to see the number of wreaths even though it was March. I noticed that one of these had been presented by friends of Cape Hill Fire Brigade and a new door of enquiry subsequently opened.

Apart from some very basic company history, I had no idea how much this brigade meant both to the company and the local area: even more, after meeting other retired firemen along with Vernon Fisher, I realized how much pride there was in the workforce.

Now a listed building, the Fire Station was opened on the 15th October 1927, some 45 years after the original formation of the Cape Hill Fire Brigade. Built by architect Spencer Wood, this building was to house both the Fire Brigade and its sister service, the Ambulance Division. These services, while principally formed to look after the health and safety of the brewery and its staff, were to play an important role in the firefighting and medical duties required around the whole borough. By the time the new station was opened the Cape Hill Brigade was recognized both nationally and internationally as a fine organization.

With his customary thoroughness and foresight, Henry Mitchell first proposed the fire brigade after becoming deeply concerned by the damage fire might do to his brewery and enterprise. Although No 2 Brewery was not completed until 1914, Henry had always urged that a future expansion should include a completely separate unit, away from existing buildings so as to minimize damage in the event of a major conflagration. When it was founded in 1882 the Brigade consisted of two officers; Supt. J. Hamilton and a Mr. Tunnicliffe, with eight men, a manual and a fire truck. From this original workforce, three attended the 1927 ceremony: R. Sherwood and T. Iownes who were pensioners of the company, and Harry Smith who was still working in the brewery after refusing to be pensioned off.

GOOD HONEST BEER

In 1885 Henry (Harry) Mitchell, serving as a lieutenant in the Smethwick Volunteer Fire Brigade, was appointed as Captain at Cape Hill and worked closely with Supt. Hamilton raising the quality and profile of the brigade which he took overseas several times for competitions such as the Paris one he had attended in 1882 as a company representative. By 1886 the first steam engine was purchased and the force expanded to 16 men.

Tragically, Harry was to contract typhoid fever and died in 1894, aged just 32 years. His father's memorials to him are part of the sporting life of Cape Hill, a later part of this work.

The brigade entered the inaugural National Steamer Trophy in 1896 and by 1903 they were able to sweep the board in all categories of that year's Earls Court Show. A Dennis motor fire engine was purchased in 1911.

Most of the brigade joined the armed forces in 1914 and the brigade was incorporated into a wider borough organization for the duration. 1924 saw the last horse used by the brigade and a new Leyland appliance, with larger pumping capacity, was purchased.

William's son, Owen, became second officer in 1924 and by 1927 the brigade consisted of three officers with 24 firemen and drivers. At the time of the 1927 opening of the new fire station, the adjoining Ambulance Division, under Superintendent Kingsnorth, had a staff of 32 personnel and were handling 2,000 medical incidents both in the brewery and in the district each year.

With the widespread bombing of British cities from 1940 onwards, the 1939-45 conflict saw the brigade in regular and challenging action. The logbooks of the time show the customary domestic emergencies, such as the fire in Windmill Lane on the 19th November 1940 which took over two hours to bring under control and a bakery fire in Waterloo Road which started at the early hour of 6.29 am on a Sunday, the 5th January 1941. There were false alarms, such as the abortive callout to the Bottlery Case Repair Shop on the 24th June 1941 illustrates. More dangerous and threatening, as a result of bombing, the brigade was called out on the 28th July 1942 and spent over five hours tackling a fire at Scribbens Bakery on Corbett Street and, two nights later, they were called out just after midnight and were at work in four separate areas of the brewery itself for over seven hours. And, of course, fires continued after the end of the bombing: six days after the allied landings in Normandy they were required to put out a badly laid fire in the main office...in June?

Both the Ambulance and Fire Divisions remained an important part of Cape Hill life after the war and right up to the final closure of Cape Hill. As well as Vernon Fisher, Barry Rowlands and Neil Willetts entertained me over two nights in March and June 2011 at The Old Swan, Netherton with tales of their days in the fire brigade. (Also known as Ma Pardoes, this fine pub brews its own excellent beer.) Some of their work was dangerous, some of it was pure routine, but there was also a more comical side.

One colleague, the winner of the big Ambulance Cup (pictured on Page 40), entered a national competition which he duly won. On his return by train to New Street he was welcomed by colleagues who had purloined a length of red carpet and a company vehicle which carried him back to Smethwick in appropriate style. Unfortunately for all concerned, they were spotted by one of the directors and all were on the carpet the following day!

And Barry, a driver for the fire brigade, told me of returning from holiday only to be called out on a 'shout' as soon as he clocked in. It all happened so quickly that his mate he was taking over from for his evening shift hadn't time to tell him that the brewery had installed raised traffic calming blocks around the yards; the ensuing rapid departure deposited both colleagues and equipment over a wide area. But the fire was put out!

The Main Gate into Cape Hill Brewery

An elderly Henry Mitchell with a dapper William Butler at the site of the new No 2 Brewery

No 2 Brewery complete and an aerial view of the Cape Hill site

The gathering at Quinton for the laying of the first stones of The William Butler Memorial Cottages. All the tradesmen gave their services free as a mark of respect. Henry and William Waters Butler are highlighted: William has a paternal hand on Owen's shoulder, Owen being the author's grandfather

The cottages have only recently been sold back into private ownership

# GOOD HONEST BEER

The Guard of Honour at the unveiling of the M&B War Memorial.
Sunday the 1st October 1922

Owen Butler commands and is seated in the centre of the front row.

Frank Townley, twice decorated, and who served with Owen in Italy, is seated fourth from the right.

A larger version of this picture can be obtained, clearly showing the names of all persons who were present.

A company picture of the M&B War Memorial

Henry Mitchell's son, Henry, known to all as 'Harry' A successful salesman for Mitchell & Co., a pioneering fireman for the company, tragically taken by typhoid fever The Harry Mitchell Leisure Centre in Smethwick was built and donated to the borough in his memory.

# GOOD HONEST BEER

The chairman inspects the M&B Ambulance Division.

A foggy morning in 1927 The new fire station pictured behind is being opened and William Waters Butler (complete with orchid) walks on the same cobbled yard where the M&B War Memorial stands today.

Overleaf: a map, close to the time of line closure showing both the railway lines into Cape Hill, although the line on the left into No2 has already been severed in places. Note that one line passes over the canal feeder, whereas the other goes under.

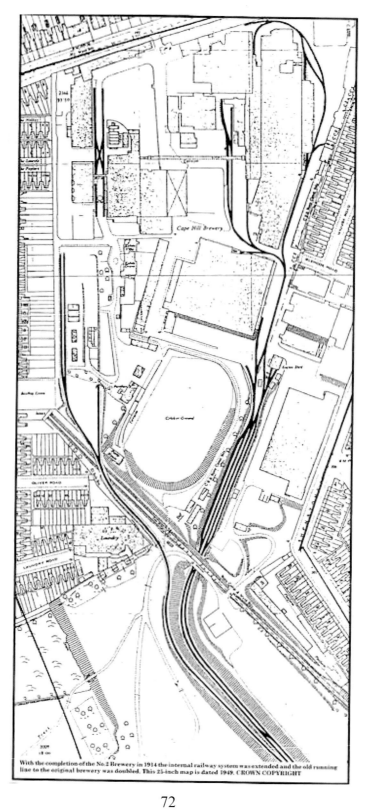

With the completion of the No. 2 Brewery in 1914 the internal railway system was extended and the old running line to the original brewery was doubled. This 25-inch map is dated 1949. CROWN COPYRIGHT

Two views of the siding into Cape Hill from the direction of Harborne. The top one taken in 1949, below in 1962

The 'Pug' and (below) Boniface waits at No 2 Brewery

Working the brewery sidings and the Curzon Street depot in 1943

Boniface & John Barleycorn: both exceptionally clean for the visitors

Women working hard at the brewery in WW1

A view of The General Office: heavily staffed in the days of pen and ink book-keeping.

Roll out the barrel! Fill up the barrel!

## SOCIAL LIFE

Over the years, sporting and social life at Cape Hill has always been an important feature.

Trips and outings have been made to all parts of the country. Our cartoon comes from the trip booklet given during the visit to the Wembley Exhibition in 1924: the remarks about the shortage of M & B beers in London are particularly pointed!

CAPE-HILLITE "WHAT REALLY IS THE IDEA OF THIS EXHIBITION GUVNOR?"
COCKNEY "TO INCREASE THE COUNTRY'S EXPORTS OF COURSE"
CAPE-HILLITE "INCREASE EXPORTS! GOOD, I SHOULD THINK THEY WANT INCREASING AN' ALL. I AINT SEEN ONE ALL DAY AND I'M AS DRY AS A LIME KILN."

A Cape Hillite puts a Londoner straight

In the days before footballers ate pasta

GOOD HONEST BEER

## THE RAILWAY

In 1903 the directors of M&B decided that they needed a railway to facilitate deliveries of malt and other essential supplies into the brewery, and to send products speedily out of the brewery and farther afield. At Burton, Bass had opened a line as early as 1859 and by 1891 had a complex of lines some 26 miles in total. This was vastly larger than M&B required.

Smethwick already had a railway station, renamed Smethwick Rolfe Street in 1963, but a glance at a map both then and now, indicates how prohibitive, if at all possible, a line would have been thence and into Cape Hill. Much closer to the brewery passed the Harborne Branch which left the main LNWR Birmingham-Wolverhampton line just north of Monument Lane. This junction was named Harborne Junction in 1879 and a single track line to Harborne itself was opened to passenger traffic in August 1874 followed by goods in the same October. Three intermediate stations, Icknield Port Road, Rotton Park Road and Hagley Road made up the line. The short journey, 2 miles and 770 yards, took 25 minutes - this time plus a history of delays dogged the passenger traffic throughout its short 60 year life, and locals used to refer ironically to their 'Harborne Express'. The terminus, Harborne, was also the site of The Chad Valley toy factory which had its own siding. Passenger traffic reached a climax of 27 trains per day in 1914, it finished completely in 1934 while the final death knell of goods traffic can be attributed to that well known agent of closure, Dr Richard Beeching. Cape Hill goods traffic finally ended on the 31st March 1962.

In 1904, after inviting tenders, M&B commissioned Gowling & Ingram to build the first, and main, section of the new line. Of interest, the original line passed under the canal feeder, while the line built later to service No 2 brewery went over it.

Just south of Rotton Park Road Station the line went under the same named road and passed under City Road (today the A4040) where the siding into the brewery commenced. The single track turned into double track and divided just past the canal feeder. A single track left turn out made its way past the cricket ground on its right where it divided again. A line went up to No 2 Brewery where there was room for two lines for shunting and storage, while two sidings were laid adjacent to the bowling green. The map on Page 72 clearly illustrates both lines. Sidings, turntables and sheds were all installed and the railway was to serve the brewery for the best part of 60 years.

Although the line has long since been dug up it is quite easy to follow as the old track bed has been used to create a walkway for local residents and school children. You can join the well signed walkway under Rotton Park Road and see quite clearly where the line into the brewery started from each direction. On one visit, a very gloomy March morning, I was privileged to be very close to a heron looking for some breakfast in one of the many pools that are on each side of the path. With a little care it is possible to identify some old railway posts amongst the overgrown banks, the bridges which were at each end of Rotton Park Road Station still stand and it is rewarding to work out the site of the platform, the sidings etc. The pumping station situated next to the canal feeder and adjoining the cricket ground still stands (2011) and, even with the readjusted levels in the land, the entry of the second line into No 2 Brewery can be envisaged. It is not an exact art, but following the line around the modern housing development makes for a rewarding if slightly eccentric way of spending a couple of hours.

The first locomotive used at Cape Hill was a 0-4-0 saddle tank built in Leeds in 1889. Originally named Frank, the engine worked at Cape Hill until 1929 under the name Beatrice. Two other locomotives, John Barleycorn and Boniface, made up the fleet, briefly complemented in the 1950s by another 0-4-0 locomotive, hired from ex-LMS stock, no. 11221 and known to the staff as 'Pug'.

This is a good place to mention the Bedford Maltings. As the name suggests, M&B had a large maltings operation in the town of

Bedford. Convenient for access to the barley growing areas of Eastern England, the buildings were situated on the junction of King's Place and Ampthill Road, adjacent to the main lines connecting London St Pancras and Birmingham. In similar fashion to the line off the Harborne branch, a 1920 rail map shows malt houses and sidings just off the Hitchin branch marked as used by M&B. For transportation brewers found it easier to soak the grain, converting it to malt, rather than move it in its original state. I have come across a letter written by M&B in June 1912 requesting permission to connect waste pipes to existing rain water pipes in order to facilitate this operation. With their own line into the brewery, M&B could move their malt literally from door to door. The staff at the Bedford Maltings was employed by M&B and the Cape Hill Fire Brigade was responsible for regular safety inspections there. On Tuesday the 15th April 1958 the Bedfordshire Fire Service was engaged at the malt house for nearly three hours tackling a blaze that started in a stationary goods wagon waiting at one of the sidings. The Bedfordshire Times & Standard reported that some 20% of the barley stored was severely damaged. Eight M&B members of staff at the malt house were jointly awarded the William Savage Memorial by fellow employees for their role in handling the fire and its consequences. B Bradbury, D Jatczak, E Apostel, C Conway, C Woodcock, M Osadciw, P Barcock and J Birch are all recorded on the shield.

GOOD HONEST BEER

SPORT AND LEISURE

Right from the start of his business enterprises, Henry Mitchell believed in the benefits of sport and we have already seen reference to his football and cricket clubs.

When his son Harry died of typhoid fever in 1894, Henry gave a cricket ground and recreation park to the borough of Smethwick in his memory. This area remains today and is part of The Harry Mitchell Leisure Centre. Happily the land is classed as 'unregistered' and the deeds are still held by the council in their original format.

The Harry Mitchell Park is a registered charity (No: 231695) and its original objectives were:

'To provide 1) A drill hall for H company of the First Volunteer Battalion of the South Staffordshire Regiment of Rifle Volunteers 2) Cricket ground for Smethwick Cricket Club 3) Such purposes in connection with gymnastics, games and recreation generally as the Council in their absolute and uncontrolled discretion shall think fit'. It is no wonder that Henry was elected as the first Freeman of the Borough in 1902.

On the 13th June 1903 the company staged a walking match from Birmingham to Droitwich. Out of 32 starters, 29 completed the 19 mile course, the winner in little more than three hours. It is not recorded whether this was a one-off event, but silver medals were awarded by the company to all those who finished the course in less than four-and-a-half hours. Certainly athletics played its part at Cape Hill, greatly encouraged by Henry Butler, and there are records of meetings and relay races, some formal, others familiar to anybody who has been roped into egg and spoon races on school sports days.

The Birmingham and District Cricket League was founded in 1888 and it seems that Henry encountered some problems with ineligible players as his company was excluded for four years from 1892. They were 1$^{st}$ X1 Champions for the first time in 1898 and were to repeat this success in 1909, 1911, and 1914. Inter-war triumphs followed in 1925, 1926, 1928 and 1931. These successful teams sometimes drew crowds of over 2,000 spectators. My grandfather, Owen Butler, played for the first team and perhaps was responsible in some small way for my life long affection for the game both as a player and follower.

The football club Birmingham St. George's reverted to Mitchells & Butlers. Young Harry Mitchell managed to get Preston North End to send a team down to Cape Hill for the opening of the ground. Given Preston's reputation at that time, it seems the equivalent of asking Manchester United to send a team today. Despite no facilities at Cape Hill, M&B entered teams into swimming galas from 1919 onwards. The bowling club opened in 1920 followed by the tennis club in 1927; both are clearly marked on the 1931 map.

As well as sport on the premises, trips were arranged for staff starting with a train trip to Margate in 1910. In 1924 a larger outing was made to London to visit the Wembley Exhibition which prompted the wonderful postcard reproduced on Page 79.

The legendary Sam Jones, lynch pin of the Tug of War team in the 1920s, was renowned for his ability to pick up quantities of beer bottle cases, all fully stocked.

GOOD HONEST BEER

A FEW FACTS, FIGURES & CURIOS

While researching this book I visited both the Coors Museum at Burton (now The National Brewery Centre) and the library in Smethwick and was able to look through a selection of ledgers, AGM minutes and all sorts of paperwork relating to both Mitchell & Co as well as M&B. I have copious notes and photocopies from looking through these volumes and have extracted just a sample from them as well as other sources to try to give an impression of the sheer volume of monies going in and out of these enterprises.

At the same time I have thrown a few figures into the mix with a view to illustrating the markets in which M&B and other brewers were operating.

Taxation on drink has always been an issue and the price of a pint has always been a balancing act for a chancellor who needs his revenue but also prizes his own political neck.

In 1887/8 tax revenue raised was £89,802,254 to which beer revenue (as opposed to revenue on all alcohol) contributed £8,721,746, or 9.71%. In the following 25 years before the outbreak of war in 1914, and not withstanding four hefty hikes in duty in 1899/90, 1894/5, 1900/01 and 1909/10, the percentage contribution of beer to overall revenues never exceeded 11.07% or dropped below 9.06%, at least until 1910 when it dropped down to 6.27%. With war and Lloyd George's hostility to the brewery trade, duties were hiked up considerably. In November 1914 beer duty alone was raised from 7/9 per barrel to 23/- and M&B, along with most of their colleagues and competitors, responded by increasing their prices. An old penny on a pint may seem 'small beer' these days but a 20% plus increase on a beer today might cause considerable comment. And, of course, once installed, these higher rates of tax were to remain in place after peace came in 1918.

GOOD HONEST BEER

In 1919-20 total liquor taxation would stand at £133,873,000, a 13.4% contribution. By the end of World War 2 the sums raised had leapt to £400,761,000 but now only 10% of the national take. And by 1976/7 the overall contribution stood at 6% but was a staggering £1,945,200,000.

The actual monies flowing in and out of Cape Hill were considerable. A 1929 picture of the General Office (page 77) shows rows of clerical staff at their desks, which in today's computer-led age appears heavily over staffed, but each person was responsible for the day-to-day running of particular pubs, or specified areas like material costs, transport etc. In 1919 the company started with £598,915 (the shillings and pence noted) on current account with Barclays Bank Ltd. During that year, Drawings were made on this account, such as 24 occasions in August when the lowest withdrawal was for £3,190 and the year finished with a balance of £629,099. Throughout the year money was kept in a deposit account with The London County & Midland which by the year end totalled £117,454.

Every penny was carefully accounted for. In 1921 it is noted that the chairman had three items of expenditure over and above his salary, two for £10 exactly and the third for 3s 6d.

Of course many other targets for duty, the motor car in particular, were to become available and beer duties as a percentage dropped but the £8,721,746 collected in 1887/8 rose to £15,882,000 in 1914/15, the two budgets the following year collected a doubling to £33,770,000 and there were two years after the war when revenues rose to £123,406,000 in 1920/21 and £121,865,000 in 1921/22. With the years of crisis, the National Strike of 1926 and the Great Crash of 1929, revenues fell but in the year of M&B's 50th birthday (1929) the duty on beer alone raised £77,151,000, with wine, spirits and tobacco added, £192,012,000, a contribution of 26.15% to the national cake.

Again in the 1929 M&B book there is a picture of the Wine and Spirit Stores under which the caption reads:

'The output of Spirits is large and the Company's brands have a high reputation. "Ballyboy" Irish whisky, "Clan Ivor", "Glenbarry", and "Dumbarton" Scotch Whiskies are special blends and are very popular. In the four local Bonded Warehouses over 400,000 gallons at full strength lie maturing in carefully selected casks. The blends are made up as Cape Hill requires. Government Duty paid by this department alone exceeds £405,000 per year'. Even in celebration the company was making a point.

What is not in doubt is that the company was profitable, very profitable, and even during the troubled years of the 1920s performed well. The company reported a profit of £528,528 in 1924, carried forward £243,807 leaving a tidy sum for investment, shares, dividends and deposit. By the end of the decade, profits had risen to £641,902 and the company carried forward £380,191. These figures were profits, not operating money: truly M&B was a very considerable concern.

In a later chapter we will look at some of the M&B estate and figures involved in building new pubs. As a national industry, the breweries spent an average of just over £1,000 per house improving their stock between 1922 and 1930 and only a quarter of their estates received attention. M&B's record during this period was considerably higher. Undoubtedly, many brewers spent a lot of money improving their buildings, but in 1928, introducing a bill in the House of Lords, Lord Balfour of Burleigh, keen on nationalization, claimed that over three quarters of the pubs in England could only be described as 'slum-pubs'. This may or not have been true. But the cost of building a new pub, probably at the expense of surrendering other licences, was high and we shall see that M&B was always aware that the return on these investments was at best steady and sometimes quite slow.

In 1860 England and Wales produced 18,316,062 barrels of beer, each containing 36 gallons. In the same year only 3,592 such barrels were imported. Domestic beer production peaked around 1900 when 32,146,769 barrels of beer were brewed. By 1920 this had slipped to

29,891,845 and by 1925 the country was importing 1,545,953 barrels of beer each year.

The price of a pint doubled from an average of 3d in 1914 to 6d by 1927. A penny on a pint at budget time would have been a large increase.

In 1969, when the author first legally bought a pint, it cost him a shilling: beer had doubled in price in 40 years. In 1976 it cost him 28p, which allowing 5p to the shilling suggest a five-fold increase in seven years. By 1985 he was charged 90p and by 2011 the 300p barrier was looming or had been passed, depending on the area of the country he found himself. In this same 40 year period the relationship in price between beer and spirits completely changed: a nip of whisky in 1969 was double the price of a pint and by 2011 there was parity. Strong drink had become cheaper, good ale had become very expensive and the beer drinker in this country had at best become the victim of a major realignment in the market.

At the current time it is fashionable to blame the supermarkets and other retail outlets for the availability of cheap drink and the worrying social consequences, especially for young people. The relationship, often testy and difficult, between government and the brewers, seems no longer to really exist. Yet in 1993, revenues raised on beer alone amounted to £4,303,000,000.

Apart from the very considerable sums of money involved in running M&B there was also the sheer volume of raw materials required to produce their beers. The company estimated in 1929 that 25,000 acres of arable land was needed to produce the barley required each year and the 1,250,000 lbs of hops they used needed an area bigger than the centre of Birmingham.

Two curios: All the time the company was seeking better ways to distribute and dispense its products. A patent agreement (No 448514) dated the 12$^{th}$ December 1934 (headed under Edward V111 despite

George V living until January 1936) shows an agreement between M&B and John Arthur Jones for rights to an invention for 'improvements in or relating to the drawing serving and delivery of beer and other liquids'. Presumably this 16 year agreement was satisfactory to both parties, but a modern patent lawyer to whom I showed this document was not convinced how well it might stand up to legal examination today.

Henry Mitchell and William Butler both used crowns as part of their company logos before amalgamating. In 1910 it was agreed to use a 'Leaping Deer' as the official trademark and it was duly registered. The logo can be seen on the beermats on page 40 and again on page 98.

CHAPTER 6: SOME COMPETITORS

Long before the time of Henry Mitchell and William Butler there had been a thriving brewing industry in Birmingham. As we saw earlier, the Plantaganet rulers of England were quick to put duty on drink and it appears that the sale of beer was regulated in Birmingham from 1166 under a royal Market Charter granted to Peter de Birmingham. The first record of a commercial brewery in Birmingham, not totally authenticated, seems to date from 1752. More definitely, Joseph Ashton opened for business in 1782 in Deritend.

Throughout the first half of the nineteenth century, and especially after the 1830 Beer Act, numerous brewery operations opened in the city, many of them small enterprises run as a secondary occupation. It is not until the 1850s that bigger operations started in response to the move of large numbers of working people from the land and into the city. Both Henry Mitchell and William Butler had rural backgrounds.

Robert Davenport started business as a small brewer in 1829. It was his son John who opened the Bath Row premises which became the home of John Davenport & Sons. When they became a limited company in 1896 they had 57 tied houses. Although a considerable presence in Birmingham for the next century, their concentration on delivering bottled beer to individual customers ('Beer at home means Davenports' was a later jingle used on television advertising) meant that they never really posed a serious threat to M&B. That said, they claimed, in 1939, to have over 250,000 customers whom they supplied from a network of small depots. In 1933 they had a 2.5% share in the domestic beer consumption market (M&B had 3.7%) and by 1938 they had increased this to 5.3% (while the M&B figure remained static at 3.7%). They were an innovative company. They returned to brewing real ales as opposed to pressurized ones in the late 1970s thus responding to the CAMRA campaigns and in 1983 won a contract with Sainsbury's to sell beer in plastic bottles. In the same year they saw off a hostile bid from Wolverhampton & Dudley

Breweries. In 1990, following a merger with Greenall Whitley, the Davenport site was closed.

A frequent theme of this book is the policy of 'fewer and better' pubs which M&B followed along with other brewers. It is interesting to note that a Davenports pub, The Black Horse, Northfield was opened in 1929 only a few hundred yards from the M&B pub, The Travellers Rest which had opened three years earlier. Even more intriguing is that the architect was the same for each pub, Bateman and Bateman. This firm was responsible for some of the largest, most sumptuous pub projects in Birmingham at this time. In 1931 they rebuilt The Australian for Davenports while The Coach and Horses at Castle Bromwich and The Tyburn House at Erdington were two projects for Ansells.

For many years Ansells were M&B's principal competitor. A former small operation brewer, Joseph Ansell opened a brewery at the junction of Litchfield Road and Park Road Aston. Artesian wells sunk below this site could produce vast amounts of good clean water and by 1890 they were rebuilding and expanding their site to meet the demands of the expanding business. Designed by Inskipp & Mackenzie, their new premises doubled capacity and additions and extensions were added in 1900 and 1906. Registered as Ansells Brewery Ltd. in June 1901, they had the assets of a freehold brewery with all its contents, 388 licensed houses and a valuation of £752,747. By 1919 they were one of 66 brewers in the country with a capitalization of between a half and one million pounds, while M&B was one of 16 with a two million plus value. Rushton's Lion Brewery was acquired in 1923 along with 100 licensed houses. The continued vitality of the company over the next 40 years enabled them and M&B to rebuild war-damaged property at modest cost under a government system set up in 1945 known as Barrelage. When they opened a new brewery in 1957 Ansells had over 1,500 tied houses. In the same year that M&B merged with Bass (1961) Ansells merged with Ind Coope and Tetley Walker, eventually becoming part of Allied Breweries. By the late 1960s they, along with M&B, and as the result of successful mergers, would be the main players in Birmingham and this situation would bring both companies into conflict with monopoly commissions. The Monopoly Commission of 1969 was especially exercised by these vast companies. Like Davenports, Ansells responded to the 1970s demand for real ale and in 1978 launched their Aston Ale. Eventually the company was brought down by poor industrial relations although Aston Manor Brewery was founded in March 1983 by four redundant Ansells workers.

Another operation in Aston, Frederick Smith Ltd., traded there from 1860 until their eventual demise in 1955. Their Model Brewery was designed by George Adlam in 1889. Perhaps taking a leaf out of the M&B book, Frederick Smith, who was knighted in 1927, sent his son to study at the Brewing School at the University of Birmingham. At one time, in 1937 they controlled over 100 houses and managed to avoid the clutches of both Ansells and M&B, although their eventual demise followed a takeover by W. Butler & Co, a long-established Wolverhampton company.

In 1878 Atkinson Brothers' Aston Park Brewery was opened as a brand new operation, followed by major expansion in 1885. Their brewery was designed by Gregory and Haynes, a Salford-based practice whose principal business was in refrigeration. By 1898 they had 80 licensed houses and continued to grow steadily over the next 50 years and eventually owned over 350 public houses. In 1959 they were bought out by M&B and the brewery was closed despite assurances to the contrary from the M&B board to the owning family, named Horton. Victor Horton was married to Edna née Butler, my great aunt.

M&B took over Homer's Vulcan Brewery in 1899, a valuable acquisition that had floated just a year earlier with 56 tied houses and a capital value of £200,000. Another enterprise eventually swallowed up by M&B was Holder's Midland Brewery. Opened in 1869 and established in Nova Scotia Street by 1879, they had doubled their tied house estate in 1900 by taking over City Brewery and their 40 properties before eventually being taken over by M&B in 1919.

As we saw earlier, there was a mass of brewery openings and closures during the late Victorian period. In 1890 the Home Office published their findings into the tied houses of Birmingham. The biggest estate belonged to the Gooch family. Based at Benacre Hall in Suffolk, the Gooch family had acquired a large plot of Birmingham land through Bishop Sherlock in 1761. Behind New Street Station today there is still both a Benacre Street and Gooch Street. Their pub estate of 159 houses was closely followed by Holt Brewery Co. Ltd with 155. (Their eventual 1934 estate of 250 houses was to be acquired by Ansells) Overall there were 74 companies controlling 1,203 houses, or, minus the two operations mentioned above, 72 companies controlling 889, an average of 12 houses each. No wonder Henry Mitchell, with 86 houses to his name, saw the opportunity to expand his company by buying up or supplying these smaller businesses.

More recently, formed in 1971, The Campaign For Real Ale, has been a competitive force throughout the industry. I still have my original CAMRA guide, a thin little book that introduced me to many fine real ales in the 1970s. Looking at their current mission statement, it seems that they and William Waters Butler had more in common than perhaps they would like to admit. Items 3 and 5 respectively state:

To support the Public House as a focus of community life

To seek improvements in all licensed premises and throughout the brewing industry

Perhaps if CAMRA had been less shrill over the past years, and keener to engage the big brewers in a more constructive dialogue, we would not have suffered the closures of so many pubs in recent years and their support for the 'focus of community life' may have been more fruitful. Undoubtedly, in the early 1970s, there was a real dearth of drinkable beer, but I cannot believe that CAMRA's founding members ever wanted the pub industry to be as centralized as it is now. Yes, there has been a welcome upturn in the number of small or micro-breweries, but the past few years have seen a depressing volume of pub closures. A later chapter on the Beer Order legislation introduced in 1989 will look more closely at this.

Finally, in 1895, in Smethwick itself, Titus Mason opened a soft drinks manufacturing company. Rather than being a competitor, it is probable that T Mason & Sons Ltd, from their nearby site in Grantham Road, complemented M&B quite well. Certainly their products were stocked side by side in local off-licences.

## CHAPTER 7: WILLIAM WATERS BUTLER

William Waters Butler was my great-grandfather. He joined the board of M&B at its inauguration in 1898, became chairman in 1914 and was still in office at the time of his death in 1939. In other words, he was directly involved and responsible for the running of a great and successful enterprise for over 40 years. He was a highly educated man who never ceased looking to improve both himself and his fellow man and was, without doubt, a pioneer of modern brewing. He was a lucky man: born in very modest circumstances, his father a fiercely ambitious man, he learnt his trade back to front, he met and worked with one of the very best Victorian brewers, Henry Mitchell, and he inherited the mantle of a great and successful business. He took the business forward, and forward through both good and bad times and when he died in 1939 left a company in excellent condition to face the years ahead.

He should not only be remembered as a successful businessman. He obviously enjoyed making money, but he recognized that his industry was not always a force for good and spent years of his life campaigning and working to make it acceptable both to government and society. His work on the Carlisle Experiment did not always endear him to his fellow brewers and we shall see he could be quite testy on the subject of taxation and what he perceived to be wrong. He gave considerable sums of money away in his life, for both educational and medical improvements, and his knighthood in 1926 was not a reward for the selling of vast amounts of beer.

William Butler's eldest son was born on the 14th December 1866 at The London Works Tavern in Smethwick. Educated at King Edward's Grammar School, William was clearly keen to join his father's company and anxious to understand all elements of his chosen profession.

Two views of a M&B Centenary Jug

An author's toy

Two M&B beermats: note the 'leaping deer' trademark.

The Shakespeare, Summer Row and Head Office, M&B, 2010 style

Two familiar faces on a wall in The Old Contemptibles, Edmund St
A magnificent exterior: The Old Royal, Church Street

The Gunmakers Arms, Bath Street:closed in 2009, open again 2011?
The Village, formerly The Roebuck, Hurst Street

Two very different bars in the same pub
The Victoria, John Bright Street

The Crown Inn, Hill Street William Butler's name still on the wall, even if covered by a Sky TV monitor!

Taken by Andy Doherty, this photograph shows the brewery in its later days from the end of Raglan Road. The lack of activity is in marked contrast to the black and white photograph on Page 144.

Robert Butler (died 1904), Burbage, Leics.
Butler brothers, William in the middle: Lodge Hill, Birmingham
Owen Butler (died 1935) lies with both his mother & father.

After finishing his schooling, William studied analytical and brewing chemistry at Burton under Professor Cartmell and then general science at The Midlands Institute where he gained medals in chemistry, hygiene and metallurgy. His two years study of theoretical and applied mechanics earned him the Siemens Medal. He also found time to study and obtain high marks in brewing, bread making and spirits manufacture via a correspondence course which seems to have resembled the modern Open University. In May 1885 his parents marked his academic achievements by presenting him with a gold watch and bookcase, some six months before his nineteenth birthday. By the time he was 21, or so he claimed later in conversation with Sydney Nevile of Whitbread, he suggested to his father that as brewer of the company he should be worth £1,000 a year and, as his father's son, a share of the company. He added that in the following year he was paid a further £3,000 from profits made. Thus as a 22 year old he was drawing £4,000 in one year (in 1888). Furthermore, Nevile suggested in his 1958 memoir that it was largely through William's persuasion that his father amalgamated with Henry Mitchell.

In addition to his Siemens Medal he received the Evans Prize in Mechanics and in 1890 wound up his studies by gaining the Silver Medal in Brewing of the City and Guilds of London Institute. This incredible all-round education was to give William a marked advantage in later years. By the time he became chairman of M&B in 1914 (aged 48) he had been chairman of the Midlands Counties Institute of Brewing and remains the only man to have chaired both The Institute of Brewing (1903) and the Brewers Society (1908) which between them represented both the wholesale distribution of beer and the manufacture of the same. His chairmanship of the Brewers Society coincided with the contentious legislation Lloyd George was attempting to pass into law. This was his first attempt to nationalize the industry and throughout 1908 any planned expansion by the brewers came to a standstill. Although the bill passed through the House of Commons, it was a remarkably ill-conceived piece of legislation with its proposals to limit all licences to a 14 year life and to ban the employment of women in pubs. The Liberal Government actually managed to get the Tory Party and the suffragettes united in opposition and the bill was defeated in the House of Lords in November. Although at a later date William was to be seriously attracted by the thought of state ownership, his vigorous workings behind the scenes, and incessant lobbying, played a considerable part in this defeat. A huge demonstration opposing the bill was organized for the 27th September in London, and four trains arrived from Birmingham alone full of would-be demonstrators. (William the agitator!)

Like his father before him, William swiftly became involved in charitable deeds and gave the Midlands Institute an annual donation of £100 to be used for the purchase of scientific books.

Active memberships of other societies quickly followed as he joined the Royal Meteorological Society, the Mineralogical Society, the Chemical Society and the Imperial Institute and the Society of Arts. His postbag must have been constantly heavy and learned as all of these societies were active publishers.

Happily he enjoyed a good social life. He and Emily Brown, a local Smethwick girl, married in 1893. Like his parents, William was married at Carrs Lane Chapel. The following year the newlyweds moved into a large property, Southfield on Norfolk Road, Edgbaston. The house was built between 1854 and 1860 for Lord Calthorpe and is situated half way down the road on the left hand side as one travels from the Hagley Road towards Harborne. At the time William bought the property the grounds extended as far as Westfield Road. The owners (in 2010), a property company, renamed it Crosby House and I understand that the house has since been sold. I have visited the house twice with the permission of the owners and was shown round by Debra Sillence who worked there and had become intrigued by both the house and its heritage. The driveway and the frontage to the house are well preserved although the kitchens appear to have been bricked up. The exquisite hall, staircase and landing are as William would have had them although the paintings on the walls are mainly of the Calthorpe family. The paintwork is strongly in the colours of Aston Villa FC, whom William actively supported. The rooms upstairs were mainly in use as modern offices and new owners face a daunting job restoring them. Returning downstairs, there is a large toilet area behind the front door: on my second visit when I was accompanied by both my wife and Vernon and Hazel Fisher, Vernon pointed out that the tiles were the same colour as the directors' toilets at the brewery: a job lot of tiles? A large room, a dining room, leads to the Orangery where William kept his collection of orchids. This vast old wooden building was leaking quite badly and needed help. The final ground floor room is vast and has a fully sprung dance floor. Apparently the room was used for a ball celebrating the accession of George V in 1910. Marble logos showing the embrace of the letters W and E, the owners William and Emily, ordain the cornices. The 1901 census shows just eight people living in this very large house: William and Emily, their two children Winifred Maud (b 1895) and Owen (b 1898), and four female domestic staff: Emily Sinwell (29) from Ulenswick and Edith Pritchard (24), Florrie Toms and Harriet Felton (both 22), all local girls. Presumably there must have been a steady flow of gardeners and other trades people either contracted or on call. The gardens, delivery bay and stables give some idea of the magnificence of the home but, all in all, it needs a tremendous amount of work.

William's collection of orchids was initially sourced from the stock of Joseph Chamberlain and he always took a dozen or so flowers with him when he watched Aston Villa and handed them out to friends. William was an active member of the Birmingham Botanical and Horticultural Society (est. 1829) and won the society's annual gold medal twice. At the time of his death in 1939, his collection was valued at £20,000.

I contacted Aston Villa FC in February 2011. Their librarian, Laura Brett, was most helpful. While William was a private attender of games, M&B were consistent advertisers both in the Villa News & Record as well as having signs inside Villa Park. William must have enjoyed the five seasons before the 1914-18 war when Villa were champions once and runners up three times.

Once on a trip to London to watch 'the Villa' he was persuaded to buy a sweepstake ticket. This unenthusiastic purchase netted William £15,000 which he promptly gave away on his return to Birmingham. Certainly he was a very wealthy man, but his generosity was remarkable. In his 70th year, it was announced at the Joseph Chamberlain Centenary meeting, held in Birmingham Town Hall on the 8th July, that he had donated £10,000 for the foundation of the Joseph Chamberlain Memorial Scholarships, open to residents of Birmingham and Smethwick to further their studies at the university. He also wiped out the debt of the Birmingham and Midland Institute by writing a cheque for the precise amount of £6,510, 18s and 3d. Recalling his parents' encouragement he said at the time: 'I am proud of the milestones in my life and still more grateful to the Midland Institute and its never-to-be-forgotten teachers, enabling me to surmount many obstacles I met in my later years'.

By the time he became Chairman of M&B in 1914 he was already a figure of some note in Birmingham. A local publication, The Searchlight of Greater Birmingham, had an occasional series entitled Imaginary Interviews. No 11 in the series, published on the 23rd January 1913, featured William Waters Butler, described as having 'a healthy countenance; vivacious and sparkling eyes; a heavy moustache, and an abundance of black wavy hair'. The 'interview' is frankly rather silly in parts but the imagined response to the suggestion of prohibition brings forth William exclaiming:

'Hang prohibition. Prohibition has proved to be an utter failure. The remedy is worse than the disease, inasmuch that instead of reducing drunkenness it actually increases it. You cannot cure a man of a habit that may be vicious by force, and if you make a law to deprive him of any pleasures in which he may indulge...he will immediately find a surreptitious method of indulging in the same pleasure or a worse substitute'.

Actually this was quite clever as William was greatly exercised by prohibition. At an AGM after the war he vigorously attacked Lord Astor who in his turn 'has charged the licensed trade with carrying on anti-American propaganda'. William continued:

'He may rest assured that America and Americans will not be unfairly criticized by the licensed trade, but when fanatical and well-remunerated Americans come over here and preach fairy tales - a stronger term could be applied - about the success of their great experiment, while disinterested persons state, and produce evidence, that it is otherwise, he must not get peevish when the licensed trade in this country aids in spreading the truth. Of course what really annoys Lord Astor is the exposure of the growing failure of Prohibition in the States. I do not want to trouble you again with my views as to Prohibition, and what it would mean if imposed upon this country, but...' (followed by comments filling a further 13 pages of the AGM minutes!)

The picture, 'The Trade', accompanied this imaginary interview (see front cover). In 1913, a year before he succeeded Henry Mitchell as chairman, it shows a vigorous, healthy man and, if the picture is to be believed, respected and liked by his peers. I have no knowledge of William's smoking habits but am informed that he was always a moderate drinker and, in later life, almost a non-drinker, although he apparently liked to taste the wine at Sunday lunch before permitting others to enjoy! Conversations I have had with those whose forbears worked at M&B confirm this autocratic style. He was obviously immensely respected by his workforce: how well known, liked or disliked is harder to ascertain. Probably it is fair to say that he was a man who reflected his times.

In the early 1920s M&B owned, including off-licences, 1,300 premises and nearly 800 of these were run by salaried managers as opposed to tenants. From their early days M&B preferred to directly control their premises. William explained this in his 1921 AGM address:

'Our preference is not because we make a retail as well as a wholesale profit…but that when managing houses we can make more certain of our patrons obtaining their supplies of goods in the best condition; we can regulate our trading operations so that prices and qualities are uniform, and at short notice can bring into early operation any regulations desired by the licensing justices or ourselves in connection with the proper conduct of licensed premises'.

His stewardship of M&B included the black years of depression including the Great Crash of 1929 and difficulties in the early 1930s. His relationship with government and with his fellow brewers, whilst always cordial, could be fraught as he was not afraid to speak his mind and always felt his first responsibility was to his company, his workforce and his shareholders. We will see how The Beer Orders in 1989 were to destroy so much of what he and his forbears had so painstakingly constructed and his annual letter to his shareholders, this one in 1931, shows how prescient he could be as well as somewhat agitated.

---

From Cape Hill on 9th December 1931

The question of the rate of Dividend upon the Ordinary Shares of the Company has required more than usual consideration this year. Your board has decided to declare the same Interim Dividend as last year, but the Directors at the same time desire to impress upon the Shareholders that in consequence of the serious fall in the present earnings of the Company, a reduction in Final dividend appears inevitable.

Although the diminished purchasing power of our patrons has affected output, the depressed position of the Brewing Industry today is mainly due to the effect of the additional Duty of 31s (£1.55 in 1931) per barrel imposed in the last Budget, which now brings the Beer Duty up to nearly 15 times the pre-War rate, and has caused an advance in wholesale and retail prices. Together with this addition of

# GOOD HONEST BEER

Duty, Income Tax was again increased, which will still further reduce our profits. These follow an increase of Duty of 3s per barrel and an increase in Income Tax during our last financial year, which together were responsible for more than our fall in profits of nearly £70,000. There was a decrease in national consumption of over 1.25 million bulk barrels, and at the same time the extortion of more than £2,750,000 from the Brewing Trade. As a contribution to relieving the financial strain upon the National Revenue, that burden was loyally borne by the Industry, and the promise made to the Chancellor that no part of the increased taxation would be passed on by the brewer to the retailer or consumer was faithfully kept.

Notwithstanding this, nearly 40% more taxation per barrel was imposed in the Emergency budget of September last and was forecasted to give a net gain to the Revenue of a further £10,000,000 per annum, and to result in a further reduction in barrelage of about 4.5 million bulk barrels. Such huge decreases in output must bring heavy financial losses upon those engaged in the Brewing and Allied Industries, Agriculture and Transport, with lower yields of Income Tax and local rates, together with much unemployment and short time among the workpeople. It acutely affects those who have investments in the Brewing Industry, for dividends will certainly have to be reduced. Furthermore, it is causing great irritation to beer drinkers who have been penalized in being singled out to bear an unfair share of national taxation by this outrageous addition to the cost of their beverage.

It is difficult to understand why this intolerable increase in the Beer Duty was ever imposed. From the Returns we have to date, there are indications that the decrease in output will exceed the estimate of the Government - the latest monthly Government Return showing a fall of nearly 27%, when compared with the same month of last years - and therefore, instead of producing an annual increase of £10,000,000, this extra Duty will probably result in a SERIOUS LOSS to the Exchequer which it cannot afford to suffer, and cause many thousands of acres now used for growing hops and barley to be thrown out of cultivation.

It is very evident that this unjustifiable increase must be taken off the Beer duty at the earliest moment. You are, therefore, earnestly requested to inform your Member of Parliament AT ONCE of the extreme urgency of the position, and press for his promise to support the rescinding of this extra Duty so unjustifiably inflicted upon an already overtaxed industry.

---

William signed this letter as Wm. Waters Butler, Chairman and did not use his knighthood as any form of lever. The baronetcy had been conferred in 1926 and the company celebrated his award by presenting him with a portrait, by Sir William Orpen R A, of the new baronet in suitable robes.

Whether William's 1931 letter achieved anything is debatable. However, the Brewers Society campaigned vigorously for a reduction in duty which Neville Chamberlain, as Chancellor, felt able to offer in April 1933. Following lengthy negotiations, duty was reduced by a considerable 35% in exchange for a reduction in the price of a pint of 1d, a small increase in beer strength, a commitment to increased output and a promise to source more home-grown barley.

Keeping these promises exercised the Brewers Society as they were concerned that beer had lost its pre-eminent position as the nation's favourite beverage, perhaps in part due to high levels of duty. Sydney Nevile of Whitbread was engaged to promote a national campaign of advertising which became known as 'Beer is Best' and ran for the six years leading up to World War 2. M&B were active participants in this scheme, while temperance activists hardly advanced their cause by scrawling the words 'left alone' on the national posters.

While William was doing his best for his shareholders there were tough decisions to make on the livelihoods of the workforce. It speaks highly for all involved that the workforce, rather than facing considerable redundancies in the challenging circumstances arising in 1932/3, accepted a six month wage cut. Whether the directors followed suit I have been unable to discover but it is difficult to imagine such arrangements being accepted today.

As well as his brewery work, William was chairman of Birmingham Cold Storage Ltd (who happened to have a big interest in the storage of hops) and was to be a lifetime governor of the University of Birmingham, after first sitting on their council from 1917. He actively promoted and collected funds to establish the Adrian Brown Professorship of Brewing at the university and donated £50,000 towards the new biological block which was opened in 1927 by Neville Chamberlain.

On his 70th birthday the Gazette recorded (the 16th December 1936)

'Sir William Waters Butler had a little family gathering at his Norfolk Road house on Monday to celebrate his 70th birthday and, of course, he received numerous messages of well-wishes and congratulations from his staff at Cape Hill and a wide circle of business friends. Everybody who has met this bighearted brewery magnate cannot fail to hold him in the highest respect. Like his brother, the late lamented Harry Butler, his numerous acts of kindness and bestowal of charity are performed unostentatiously. He hates the limelight'.

The reporter continued: 'the other week I saw him at St. Andrew's in the company of Sir Percival Bower, Sir James Curtis and Alderman A.H. James. He had his hat full of the inevitable orchids clipped from the plants which at one time were the pride of Joseph Chamberlain at Highbury. Everyone in his circle at a football match must wear a choice bloom. One must sympathize greatly with Sir William for the severe blows he has received of late years through losses in his family and among his closest business associates. However a birthday celebration is not the occasion on which to dwell on these sorrowful events. So to Sir William, on behalf of all my readers, I tender whole hearted wishes for many more years of happy and contented life'.

Two family deaths are alluded to above. His brother, Henry Alexander, more generally known as Harry, died in 1933. Born in 1870 Harry was an active sportsman and had been successful at school in athletics and cycling. Like William he joined his father at the brewery, became a managing director and was also inclined to give monies to worthy causes. In 1927 he sent £4,500 as a contribution to the National Playing Fields Association and this sum was used to purchase the site of what became the Kingston Hill Recreation ground. A cinder track was laid for use by the Small Heath Harriers of which Harry was chairman, but local children consistently vandalized the site and it quickly closed. Perhaps William, given his support for Aston Villa, delighted in pointing out the ground's proximity to St. Andrews, home of arch rivals Birmingham City.

Even closer to home, William lost his son, Owen, in 1935. Owen, my grandfather, died in slightly strange circumstances on a yacht at Cowes. Despite some family uneasiness as to the cause of his death, I am satisfied that, after a slightly over strenuous run back to his yacht, following some time rowing against a strong tide, he collapsed and failed to regain consciousness. There is some evidence from the coroner's report that gas may have leaked from a stove, but I think Owen was basically unlucky. On his death, his father bequeathed £1,000 to the 5th Battalion, the Royal Warwickshire Regiment in which Owen had served in both France and Italy. His obituary noted that he left a wife and two daughters which was actually incorrect as my grandmother was carrying their third child at the time.

When I first visited his house, I showed photographs of William to some of the staff working there. My physical likeness to William was commented on. Also I was told that there was something slightly odd about the main staircase. They had all, at some time or other, tripped or fallen on it. I am not superstitious, nor especially spiritual, but I could not resist telling them that Sir William had indeed collapsed and died on that very staircase, which caused a little flutter. William suffered a heart attack on his way upstairs to bed and died on the 5th April 1939.

Amongst the numerous obituaries, I was intrigued by one from The Gazette which suggested he was the licensee of The Crown in Broad Street in 1875. As he would have been nine at the time, I swiftly deduced that the writer had confused his generations. More importantly, William's death was noted at both local and national level. The Times said of him that 'he would never be a party to anything connected with the trade which he did not feel was in the public interest'. I personally think, above all, William was concerned with the interests of his company, that he was primarily a businessman. His great success was in working closely with the authorities, always keeping abreast of the political will of the day, and his policy of 'fewer and better' allowed his company to prosper within the financial and social constraints imposed. A tribute published a month after his death developed this theme:

'Sir William was as proud of Birmingham as he was of the beer he brewed: he was a princely benefactor to innumerable good causes and above all to the University of Birmingham. With his shrewd practical sense he could produce a working model out of an ideal. He became a pioneer of the improvement of public houses, and being what he was, he could hardly have done otherwise. Before improvement was practiced on a large or municipal scale anywhere else Sir William had convinced the Birmingham magistrates that better public houses, better distributed, were due to their city. The co-operation between the licensing justices, under the chairmanship for many years of Mr George Bryson, and the brewers became fruitful as well as amicable. The policy of Fewer and Better grew steadily in fame and Sir William was its inventor'. George Bryson, himself, whose term of office lasted from 1921 until his retirement in 1944, commented:

'I am now in my 18th year as chairman. It is not too much to say that throughout the whole of that time Sir William has been a constant help to the committee. Moving about the country as I do, amongst other licensing authorities, I find we have a very high reputation in Birmingham for the way in which the licensing business is conducted. In a large measure this is due to the example and the influence of Sir William Waters Butler. He is the coiner, I believe of the phrase, 'Fewer and Better', and in his own business as well as in his influence in the Trade generally he has always been anxious not only  to carry out that slogan to the letter but in the spirit also'.

William's final Will was published on the 13th May 1939, the net value being £534,472. As well as providing for his family, he bequeathed sums of money and shares for M&B to use for the upkeep of the homes of M&B pensioners. He left various educational grants totalling £4,000, and just over £5,000 to medical establishments in the city. It is fair to note some vanity in these bequests as twice he stipulated that a bed he endowed was to be named "The Sir William Waters Butler Bed", but, as in life, in death he spread himself widely and generously.

In 2011, and onwards, a Sir William Waters Butler award is still awarded to the best third-year student in Brewing and Distilling at Heriot Watts. A prize of books worth £150 is presented at the annual dinner of the Scottish section of The Institute of Brewing and Distilling. Lady Butler bequeathed this award on her death in September 1950 following the closure of the facility in Birmingham.

William was buried in the same vault as his son, Owen, and lies next to his brothers. The modern visitor to Lodge Hill Cemetery can visit the site. Entering the cemetery at the junction of Weoley Park Road and Weoley Avenue, a short walk up the drive of a few hundred yards brings you to a gap in the trees on the left. The graves are a further one hundred yards up this covered walkway.

CHAPTER 8: THE CARLISLE EXPERIMENT

At the outbreak of war in 1914 licensing changes were swiftly introduced. In August, powers to close pubs and to restrict their opening hours were given first to the military authorities and later to the civil ones. By October London's closing time had changed from 12.30am to 10.00pm and the following year most pubs in the United Kingdom were required to be closed by 9.30pm.

As his failed 1908 Licensing Bill had shown, Lloyd George was always hostile to the breweries, which he perceived as having too much power. Politically he was a temperance supporter although his support can always be shown to have been 'convenient'. In 1915 he suggested that 'drink is doing us more damage than all the German submarines put together'. There was evidence that drunkenness and absenteeism were affecting some of the munitions industry with a shortage of ammunition resulting. Lloyd George was ideologically inclined to nationalize the brewing industry and formed the Liquor Central Control Board (LCCB) in June 1915. This government quango consisted of 16 members and was appointed by the Minister of Munitions with a brief to control alcohol sales and consumption where it was felt necessary. When the board convened there was just one representative of the brewing industry present: S.O. Nevile of Whitbreads. A further brewer was appointed in January 1916: William Waters Butler. Chaired by Lord d'Abernon, amongst the other 13 members was Joseph Chamberlain's son, the future Prime Minister, Neville.

The area around Carlisle, one of the biggest munitions towns in England, gave its name to the LCCB's work known after as The Carlisle Experiment. Five breweries were taken over by the state at a cost of £900,000 as well as 235 licensed properties.

The board's brief was to lower consumption by restricting trading hours, Sunday closing and by tighter credit terms. Spirit sales were to be banned in certain areas. Further, landlords were to be paid fixed salaries which were to be increased by commission on the sales of food and non-alcoholic drinks.

Prior to the 1914-18 War, pubs had been allowed to stay open during the day. Afternoon closing was enforced from 1915 and stayed largely in force for the next 60 years. This led directly to the short Sunday lunchtime session of noon-2pm which was a standard part of British life for so long and was once memorably described to me as 'two hours frenetic desperation'. A similar regime in Australia, curtailing evening opening hours, was known as the 'five o'clock swill'.

Undoubtedly, in a wartime situation, the LCCB had considerable success. Overall drunkenness fell dramatically in the war years and, in Carlisle alone, the 953 cases heard in 1916 fell to 320 in 1917 and just 80 the following year. Although this was welcome, there was evidence that the state-run breweries produced beer of a lower quality (at a higher price) which later led to William being asked, along with his colleague, Nevile, to examine the whole beer process (in 1922). They were to report that there were problems at every stage of production: doubtless William's knowledge of chemistry and brewery science facilitated these discoveries.

As well as in Carlisle, the Board used their powers to take state control of properties near the ordnance factory at Enfield Lock and the naval base at Invergordon. The Enfield Lock pubs were released back into private hands in 1923 but the situation in Carlisle was not fully resolved until 1974.

The 1921 Licensing Act transferred the assets of the LCCB to the Home Office.

Involvement in The Carlisle Experiment was to have a major impact on the thinking of William Waters Butler and for a while brought him into some conflict with his fellow brewers.

GOOD HONEST BEER

M&B's sales during the 1914/15 winter fell dramatically, although the acquisition of Cheshire's Brewery helped soften the impact of this one third reduction. As new chairman, William Waters Butler reminded his shareholders in 1915:

'The net decrease in the barrelage is equal to the barrelage you acquired by the purchase of the Cheshire's brewery, so you can readily understand how much greater would have been the increase in the cost of production at Cape Hill, with its heavy fixed charges, if you had not acquired that additional barrelage'.

William's co-brewer on the committee, Sydney Nevile, suggested that his colleague was totally opposed to state control and quoted him as saying: 'They'll buy my brewery over my dead body'. However, meetings with Lloyd George and other members of the board seems to have altered his opinions. It will never be known quite what drove this conversion but it is reasonable to assume that William Butler was, more than anything, protecting his own interest. He could see that the government was determined, if it could, to drive through a form of nationalization and that he was probably better off being a part of that programme, rather than carping from the edges. However, it soon became clear to everybody that the government was in no position to finance this programme and that alcohol revenues were rapidly increasing, a situation preferable to running a state owned non-profit making pub trade and William's enthusiasm rapidly waned.

But in 1916 at a shareholders' meeting he said:

'The trade has had to spend most of its time battling with those who would rob it of lawfully-acquired assets, and has been so restrained or regulated that it has been unable to afford, under the best conditions, all the facilities the customers require for their reasonable refreshment and recreation… What a different licensing world we should have seen today had the owners and licensees during the past 30 years have been granted the privileges in connection with the improvement of licensed premises of which the Central Control Board is making such good use'.

Whatever the eventual outcome, here William was totally committing himself and his company to the 'fewer and better' policy. He attacked what he perceived to be bad business practice by many smaller concerns and, again justifying his belief in state control, claimed that many of his colleagues would accept this control on the correct terms:

'The constant irritation caused by would-be reformers, the oppressive, coming very close to vindictive, taxation imposed, the varying administration of the licensing laws throughout the country, the unfair references made in connection with the calling and to those engaged in it, make many feel they would be prepared to take up a more peaceful occupation'.

Henry Mitchell had once claimed that his beer was not, in any way, a contributor to drunken behaviour. (see Page 46) Perhaps William, like his predecessor, was guilty of overcooking his argument. In fact, despite much evidence to the contrary, the war years were kind to the brewers. Bass, Ratcliff and Gretton Ltd reported net profits in 1914/15 of £258,800 and £344,600 in 1916/17, a 25% increase, while M&B's profits rose by 20% in the same period. Of course many thousands of young men were away fighting for their country, but there was still left a vast workforce which was required for the war effort itself and the day to day running of the country. Government interference, especially in the area of opening hours, was an irritant.

As early as 1915 William suggested that:

'...the working man would not be regulated by so-called temperance reformers as a child, and then afterwards be appealed to as a hero by the enlisting sergeant, and he will not give you long working hours if he is to be told that after a hard day's toil he is to go home and not think of a glass of beer or recreation. Treat him as a man and he will act as such, but if by petty and irksome restrictions you make him sulky, then there is trouble'.

Addressing his shareholders in 1918, William acknowledged this wartime growth and, as usual, threw in his three penny worth as regards taxation.

'Four years ago on the outbreak of war no one in the brewing trade anticipated that it would prosper as it has done, for not only have the sound concerns such as our own company exceeded pre-war profits, but owing to the unequal and unfair operation of the Excess profits duty, brewing companies which in pre-war days were unable to pay dividends have now so greatly improved their financial positions as to give the impression that the brewing trade is not only highly prosperous but is now able to bear a rate of taxation far in excess of any rate that would have been dreamt of in peacetime'.

Many pubs were rebuilt in Carlisle and several new ones constructed. An architect, Harry Redfern, was responsible for several of these and it is interesting to note that Redfern and his designs were admired by William. He particularily approved of designs made for The Malt Shovel and The Apple Tree in Lowther Street, The Coach and Horses, Kingstown and The Crown, Stanwix, all of which have marked similarities to some M&B designs which we will see in the next chapter.

Lloyd George most certainly achieved remarkable results supplying the armed forces with munitions and equipment, but the weaker beer produced during this time was not popular and industrial strikes in the shipbuilding industry late in the war were largely resolved when more lenient access to beer was reintroduced.

In 1917 a Devon-born comedian, Ernie Mayne, recorded a song, 'Lloyd George's Beer'. The words are reprinted below and a free original recording is available on the internet.

# GOOD HONEST BEER

We shall win the war, we shall win the war,
As I said before, we shall win the war.
The Kaiser's in a dreadful fury,
Now he knows we're making it at every brewery.
Have you read of it, seen what's said of it,
In the Mirror and the Mail.
It's a substitute, and a pubstitute,
And it's known as Government Ale (or otherwise)

Lloyd George's Beer, Lloyd George's Beer.
At the brewery, there's nothing doing,
All the water works are brewing
Lloyd George's Beer, it isn't dear.
Oh they say it's a terrible war, oh law,
And there never was a war like this before,
But the worst thing that ever happened in this war,
Is Lloyd George's Beer.

Buy a lot of it, all they've got of it.
Dip your bread in it, Shove your head in it
From January to October,
And I'll bet a penny that you'll still be sober.
Get your cloth in it, make  some broth in it,
With  a pair of mutton chops.
Drown your dogs in it, pop your clogs in it,
And you'll see some wonderful sights (in that lovely stufo.)

Lloyd George's beer, Lloyd George's Beer.
At the brewery, there's nothing doing,
All the water works are brewing,
Lloyd George's Beer, it isn't dear,
With Haig and Joffre when affairs look black,
And you can't get at Jerry with his gas attack.
Just get your squirters out and we'll squirt the buggers back,
With Lloyd George's Beer.

The Carlisle Experiment was probably, in the extremis of war, justifiable. At the outset, Lloyd George was certainly hoping to be able to nationalize the industry and, for a while at least, seems to have convinced William Waters Butler that this was no bad thing. The closeknit working together of the committee, the frank and open exchange of views and opinions, seems to have paved the way for a less confrontational platform on which the brewers and government could work together. William's flirtation with nationalization certainly irritated many of his colleagues in the trade but the policy of 'fewer and better' came to fruition as a result of this work and was to be of benefit to any brewery looking to expand in the post-war years.

For a fuller history of The Carlisle Experiment, Olive Seabury wrote a book published in 2007: The Carlisle State Management Scheme which is available from her publisher (see bibliography).

CHAPTER 9: THE M&B PUB ESTATE AND SOME CASE
STUDIES

'Fifty years ago the generality of public houses, especially in the towns, stood on rather a low level'.

'Apart from its primary function as a place of refreshment the improved public house is a place where a man may cross his legs and have his talk out, air his opinions, forget the galling restraints of the day and speak and act with freedom...Why not, then in good surroundings, in clean airy rooms, in decency and in comfort'.

These two extracts from M&B's 1929 celebratory book Fifty Years of Brewing sum up the policy of the company precisely, even hinting that few decent pubs existed before the formation of M&B.

The period immediately after the war saw a short-lived boom but the brewers found they were operating in a very different climate to that of pre-1914. The gravity or strength of beer had been considerably reduced during the war years and high levels of taxation allied to increased prices for the raw materials needed for the production of beer dissuaded brewers from restoring higher gravity beer. By 1920 William Butler noted that 'the public have now grown accustomed to weaker beers'. Although the government and the temperance movement had retreated from their assault on the industry, the brewers knew that there was no question of longer opening hours and that their establishments were regularly inspected for any perceived breakdown in generally acceptable behaviour. Socially, drunkenness, rather than a mark of male virility, was becoming something squalid and undesirable and there were more ways of amusing oneself other than standing at a bar. The cinema became an attractive alternative to the pub, more money was spent on tobacco products and there was a doubling of allotment holders in the immediate post-war period.

The policy of 'fewer and better' pubs that William and his board actively pursued saw the building of several show case establishments during the 1920s. His son, Owen, was actively engaged in this programme, although I have come across some evidence that he spent a little too much time with one of the architects engaged in rebuilding and designing his own private residence in the village of Belbroughton. On returning from war in 1918, Owen had spent time learning different aspects of brewery business but, specifically, he became involved in the survey department responsible for building and rebuilding premises and was to be responsible for over 70 new builds during his career.

In order to get permission to build a new pub there were several hoops through which the brewer was required to jump. Legally, magistrates were inclined only to grant permission for a new site to be developed if other licences had been surrendered. M&B were looking to develop sites away from the city centre, on crossroads and junctions in surburban locations. In 1927 alone M&B surrendered over 300 licences. The cost of building a new pub usually came in at about £25,000 during the 1920s and the outlay of such sums did not guarantee a quick return. William's address to the 1928 shareholders' meeting included the following observation:

'You must not assume that the opening of new licensed premises in new districts is at once a profitable venture – that is by no means always the case; the building and equipping of new premises can only be done at a very considerable outlay, to which must be added the cost of the land and the cost of the licences removed and surrendered as a condition of the new grant. It is often some years before the company obtains an adequate trading profit from a new property, but this policy does ensure our retaining trade which might otherwise be lost by the transference of population to a new district'.

In that same year, 1928, M&B raised, by share issue, £600,000 purely to have funds available for their building programme, an exercise repeated just before William's death in 1939 when a further £535,000 was realized.

# GOOD HONEST BEER

When M&B published their book, Fifty Years of Brewing 1879-1929, the reader could feel palpable pride leaping off the pages. The particular pubs they highlighted were flagship designs and all recently built.

The Travellers Rest, Northfield
The Stockland Inn, Erdington
The Yew Tree Inn, Yardley
The Antelope, Sparkhill
The British Oak, Stirchley
The Brookhill Tavern, Alum Rock
The White Horse Hotel, Congreve Street.

M&B were very proud of these pubs in 1929; by 2010 there had been a marked change in their circumstances. These seven pubs are all illustrated in the section of photographs between pages 129 and 144.

The Travellers Rest was designed with a thatched roof by Architects Bateman & Bateman and opened on the 21$^{st}$ May 1926. Situated northof the now demolished Longbridge plant, it sat on the junction of Bristol Road South and Bell Lane. A roof fire in July 1941 closed the business for four months and an off-licence was added in 1954. The pub was still trading in 2002 but now lies under The Grosvenor Shopping Centre.

The Stockland Inn, another Bateman and Bateman project, was opened on the 24th November 1924 at a cost of £22,850. Standing at the Marsh Hill and Streetly Road junction in Erdington, this building was promoted by M&B postcards. No longer trading as a pub, the new owners run a very smart and popular Chinese restaurant. The owners, Modern China, have an excellent website, and there are lots of customer recommendations posted on the internet. The building itself is still recognizable from its M&B days and in excellent condition.

GOOD HONEST BEER

The Yew Tree Inn closed in 2000 and was demolished to make way for shops. The closure was enforced by a court order following police complaints of rising crime at and around the pub. There were two arson attacks immediately after the closure combined with obvious local tensions. The shops currently on site form The Yew Tree Centre and there is a licensed premises of the same name. Originally opened on the 22$^{nd}$ January 1926, The Yew Tree Inn was designed by James & Lister Lea.

The Antelope, Sparkhill is a striking building at 512 Stratford Road at the junction with Baker Street. Designed by H.W. Hobbiss there is a sundial on the Baker Street side of the building with the cheery notation: 'I tell the bright hours only'. Opened on the 17$^{th}$ April 1924, a sculpture of an antelope was added in 1929. This was designed by William James Bloye, who, influenced by Eric Gill, worked in and around Birmingham before and after the 1939-45 war. The feature itself was sculpted by Tom Wright. At one time M&B owned and sub-leased some shops at either end of The Antelope. The building today looks in very good condition and is a Balti restaurant.

The British Oak, Stirchley on Pershoe Road was rebuilt by M&B in 1926 from a design by Mr. Brassington of James & Lister Lea. A terrace and bowling green were included and the assembly room could sit over 50 diners. When I passed there recently the pub was advertising real ales, live music and was promoting a building 'full of character…set in an ideal location…well stocked bar full of fairly priced beers and a warm welcome'. Sounds like a good pub to me…

Another pub still trading in 2010, The Brookhill Tavern,n is on Alum Rock Road in Saltley on the junction with Brook Hill Road. Following enquiry, I understand that midweek trade is usually quite slow but lively at weekends. It was a showcase M&B pub when it opened on the 20$^{th}$ January 1928 designed in a Jacobean style by G. B. Cox. The original gardens were most impressive.

GOOD HONEST BEER

The last pub I have listed in this section was built earlier. When M&B reopened The White Horse in 1906 after restoration by West Bromwich architects Wood and Kendrick it must have been one of their showcase establishments as they spent over £17,000 on the building alone. As well as bars, there were function rooms where societies could meet and they had one room capable of seating up to 150 people. The White Horse Hotel closed in 1965 to make way for a new library.

William Waters Butler: a successful brewery executive in his prime

Two boardroom gatherings: Taken in 1933 Owen sits opposite a frail looking William (who indeed had been seriously ill) and below, stands behind his father

Owen Butler with his second daughter, Jill, the author's mother

Owen Butler and unknown friend in almost matching suits

The Apple Tree Inn, Lowther Street, Carlisle Designed by Harry Redfern and much admired by William Waters Butler
Below: A Redfern floor plan.

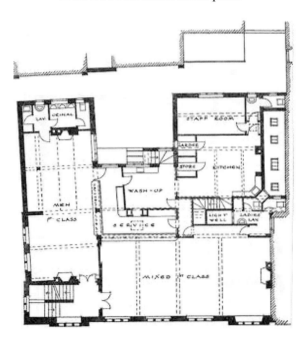

The Black Horse, Northfield A Davenports Pub, perhaps also influenced by Redfern. This design by Batemans who also worked closely with M&B

Floor plan below

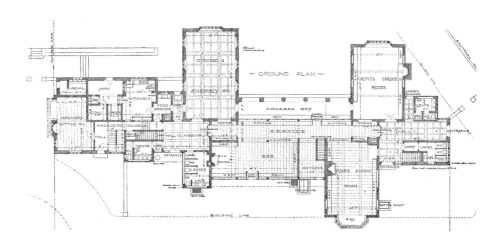

The Travellers Rest, Northfield: before and after a M&B rebuild

The Stockland Inn, Erdington with ornamental gardens.
A successful Chinese restaurant in 2011.

The Yew Tree, Yardley and The Antelope, Sparkhill

The British Oak, Stirchley: before and after...

The British Oak again: take one backyard and hey presto!

The Brookhill Tavern, Alum Rock. The interior shot shows
ashtrays but little else to distract the customer from his pint

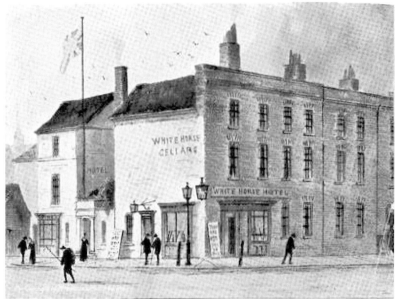

The White Horse Hotel in 1882, rebuilt by M&B in 1906, became
The White Horse in Congreve Street; it closed in 1965

William with a M&B cricket team: looking unusually disinterested
Perhaps his tax demand had arrived that morning
The magnificent M&B ground with a good crowd in attendance

Who dropped the spud?
A victorious M&B football team, circa 1932

Anyone for tennis?
A cracking night out!

M&B Brewery,Cape Hill.1962

A view of the brewery from the lower end of Cape Hill in 1962

The terraced houses and clearly shown café are all long gone as can be seen in the colour picture on Page 103.

There appears to be much more of a sense of community here, even though the pram looks curiously unattended.

Standing on exactly the same spot in 2011, looking up Cape Hill, is a very different experience.

# CHAPTER 10: A CENTRAL BIRMINGHAM TOUR

This chapter is a slight departure. In most of his tragedies, Shakespeare had a lighthearted scene, now referred to as comic relief. Perhaps what follows is part of that tradition but, hopefully, is also relevant to the book as a whole.

As will be obvious, I am not from Birmingham. I have got to know Smethwick, Edgbaston and Harborne but apart from a few trips to Broad Street and the Central Library, I am ignorant of the city centre. As I prepared this book I thought it would be useful to try to get to know this area a little and decided that the obvious way to do that was to organize a walk, visiting some M&B pubs. By the very nature of time, the trading situation in each of these pubs may have changed since my visit.

Consequently, I contacted Vernon Fisher who suggested I write down the name of a few pubs that I might like to visit and he would work out a journey plan. I spent an evening with Andrew Maxam's excellent 2002 book Time Please!(see bibliography) Concentrating on the central area, I eventually came up with 11 names and in the order I originally noted them, I sent this list to Vernon:

Red Lion (now Old Royal) 53 Church Street
Westward Ho (now O'Neills) 232-5 Broad Street
Shakespeare Tavern 4 Lower Temple Street
Victoria 48 John Bright Street
Old Contemptibles 176 Edmund Street
Shakespeare Inn 31 Summer Row
Roebuck 152/154 Hurst Street
Gunmakers Arms 92 Bath Street
White Tower (now Moriarty's) 126 Lawley Street
Trocadero 18 Temple Street
Crown Inn Hill Street

# GOOD HONEST BEER

When Vernon rang me a few days later at my home in Devon, he confirmed that he had made a plan but requested that I did not expect him to drink in every pub. That proviso agreed, we set off one April morning and I offer this tour, not as a final word, but as a thoroughly worthwhile and enjoyable rummage through the entrails of M&B.

A short bus journey from Harborne, the best way to see any city, deposited us at the top of Broad Street. Strolling down, we passed William Butler's The Crown and the now demolished Crown Brewery, before stopping briefly at the Hall of Memory at the far end of Centenary Square. Vernon took me past Baskerville House before making way to Summer Row and our first stop, The Shakespeare Inn, on the junction with Lionel Street. This is a beautiful old pub and obviously still very much part of the current M&B estate. As it was still barely 11 o'clock we decided on tea and coffee while talking to a young bar person who was making his way up through the company and who told me something of the current training programmes etc. The bars and rooms were spotless and beautifully laid out in a slightly old-fashioned manner.

We walked round the corner from Summer Row to Fleet Street where the current incarnation of M&B has its head office. The building is very new and open planned. In the foyer is a magnificent old clock, a wedding gift from a Butler to a Mitchell. We were shown round the building, met a few people and I had a brief glimpse of the current boardroom with familiar portraits hanging on the wall, including the Orpen portrait commemorating William's baronetcy.

Our next scheduled visit was to Bath Street and The Gunmakers Arms. This is quite a long walk through not the smartest part of the city and, as the pub itself is no longer trading, might be considered an avoidable trek. As I have said this is a personal view and I found it worthwhile. Andrew Maxam in Time Please! (see bibliography) describes The Gunmakers Arms thus: 'the name of the pub reflected the predominant industry in this area, a former Atkinson's pub that still thrives today'. Not in 2010, but the building itself with its smart red livery still gives off a feeling of something good and prosperous although the legal papers and the closed curtains round the door were a little depressing. (Happily I understand there is to be a reopening in 2011.)

We now made our way back down to the junction of Edmund Street and Livery Street and to one of the highlights of the day. The Old Contemptibles is the personification of a proper pub. On the day I visited it with Vernon we were still at the tea/coffee stage but I and my wife have since remedied this by having a most enjoyable pub lunch there and plan more of the same on our future visits. Quite apart from the splendid Victorian décor, there are some fine illustrations depicting the First World War, the 'Contemptibles' and, to my great pleasure and surprise, two pictures I instantly recognized of Henry Mitchell and William Butler. The young lady serving at the bar had no idea about the two old boys on the wall but expressed interest in my ramblings and I think was actually quite intrigued.

Just down the road, on the junction of Church Street and Cornwall Street stands the Old Royal. Originally The Red Lion, this magnificent building is still busy trading. A different atmosphere to the OC, perhaps aimed more at a younger market, I was a little disappointed but I'm sure it thrives.

Vernon and I now moved towards New Street Station passing The Trocadero in Temple Street followed by The Shakespeare Tavern in Lower Temple Street. Knowing we still had a lot of ground to cover, we walked past these pubs quite quickly, stopping long enough to take pictures of their exteriors and to note the ghastly yellow of The Shakespeare. The building next to this pub, now a sportswear shop, was once part of the much larger premises.

Stopping briefly to watch the trains entering and leaving New Street, (another passion), we moved on to one of William Butler's own pubs, The Crown on the junction of Hill Street and Station Street. The exterior is remarkably preserved and despite the Sky TV and other promotions inside, it is possible to imagine rows of Victorian folk supping their ale along the vast old bar which still features some original fittings. William Butler's name still adorns the wall, even if hidden behind a vast television screen. Compared to The Shakespeare Inn and The Old Contemptibles it seemed quite run down and it certainly smelt of stale beer.

Talking of which, Vernon and I were now working up quite a thirst and I had had enough tea for one morning. So, following a long walk down Hurst Street to The Roebuck, now renamed The Village, we decided to have a little 'stop'. Hurst Street is a thoroughfare full of contradictions: on one side of the road are the National Trust back-to-back houses attracting tourists, while on the other side I saw a young man vomiting outside a bar, and it was only 11.15 am. From pictures I had gathered, The Village seems to have had a new window installed recently but neither Vernon nor I felt especially tempted to go in. I did notice a planning application dated March 2010 for chairs and tables outside but couldn't quite see the attraction of sitting opposite a garage full of cars.

After a few disappointments I was pleased to find The Victoria on a corner site linking Station Street and John Bright Street. Although I am quite a traditionalist when it comes to pubs, I do like finding original ones and The Victoria is certainly that. The dark green exterior is not especially eye grabbing and the entrance lobby gives no idea of what awaits you, except there are many music posters and pictures on the wall. Step inside and on the right is an old-fashioned Victorian bar where Vernon photographed me. Next door is a garish music bar with amazing cartoons painted on the walls. The barman was flamboyant, good to watch as he served his drinks, and a mid-day gin and tonic slipped down a treat. Apparently the night-time trade at The Victoria is pretty lively and it was certainly fun to visit.

We now slipped down to the canal. The whole area has been redeveloped in recent years and I'm sure many people enjoy a stop at one of the many bistros or restaurants that have sprung up.

# GOOD HONEST BEER

Broad Street beckoned. Filtering our way through a near-deserted shopping mall, we made our way back to The Crown, now a 1980s themed nightclub. Closed at this time of the day, Vernon was adamant that William Butler would not have approved of the current décor. Still the outside is well worth a look.

Finally, up the road to O'Neills, formerly The Westward Ho. As its name suggests, a strong Irish theme predominates and the bar is fully stocked, brightly lit and appealing. We were made welcome and enjoyed an excellent, good value lunch of jacket potatoes and fish pie. Vernon finally managed to get round a good pint of real ale while I kept him company with a large glass of Australian rose: did I hear Sir William stirring in his grave?

At the end of this tour I reflected on each of the pubs we had visited. Each of them had their own character, atmosphere and was, happily, individual. I think being a stranger to the city may have been to my advantage as I had no preconception of what I might find. As a whole, I thoroughly enjoyed going to these pubs. Back in 1933 a director of Truman Hanbury Buxton deplored the loss of personal service in large pubs and noted that people preferred to order drinks at the bar and the Royal Commission on Licensing agreed that people seem to prefer 'perpendicular drinking', like preferring to stand watching football. Or perhaps they were simply advocating horizontal drinking! In 2010 I found the service both good and friendly.

Each person has their view on a pub and my opinion is of no greater value than any other. A year after my tour, I met three ex-M&B firemen in a Black Country pub and we all agreed that the good beer, quiet parlour atmosphere, the highly polished tables and chairs and the lack of piped music, all added up to a perfect place for a quiet evening's chat. Perhaps those very qualities would put off some people but I don't think any of us would like to return to the days of spittoons, while the smokers have probably been sidelined for ever.

GOOD HONEST BEER

The whole tour took a little over four hours, including our short breaks and lunch. It gave me an excellent introduction to the city centre and a few of its pubs.

I took a lot of photographs during this walk. Space and cost dictate that only some of them could be used for this book and they can be found in the second section of colour illustrations starting on page 97.

# CHAPTER 11: ANOTHER WAR AND THE YEARS OF PLENTY

Shortly after William Waters Butler's death in 1939, M&B acquired the Highgate-Walsall Brewery Co.Ltd. This added a new estate of houses in Walsall, an area close enough to Cape Hill for supply and a place where M&B had little presence. In deference to the locally popular dark mild ale, the Walsall brewery was kept in full production.

The 1930s had seen a resurgence in beer drinking. Large increases in beer duty in 1930 and again in 1931 (which exercised William so much) led the brewers to promote their products in a national advertising campaign that ran until the outbreak of war. 'Beer is Best' was the campaign slogan and advertised both the product and the pub. A marked side effect of this campaign was the large increase in the drinking of bottled beer. By 1938 bottled beer accounted for 25% of all beer consumed. M&B's beer sales reflected this trend. In 1936 they were selling over 20 million bottles of 'Cape Ale' a year.

Women again played a large part in the running of the brewery during the 1939-45 conflict. One lady dray worker continued to work after 1945 her only stipulation being that she would not tolerate bad language. Yet again many of the male workforce were serving in the armed forces and a further 33 names were to be added to the memorial by the end of World War 2, comprising of both servicemen and victims of enemy bombing.

Beer duty soared. It doubled in 1939, and by 1944 had increased by some 500% but generally the wartime coalition was reasonably well disposed to the breweries and keen to supply the armed forces. Churchill himself responded to a request for more beer during the 1944 campaign in Italy, saying: 'Good. Press on. Make sure that the beer – four pints a week – goes to the troops under the fire of the enemy before any of the parties in the rear get a drop'. In Birmingham the local licensing panel was 'reluctant to do anything which might tend to separate the working man from his mug of beer', a very different approach to the pious leanings of the earlier conflict.

One interesting result of both conflicts was that pre-tax profits soared at the breweries. In wartime, investment and the upkeep of property came to a halt. Indeed, the immediate period of austerity after the wars, coupled with much restriction imposed on output, was more challenging.

The different nature of this war, with its indiscriminate bombing of cities and civilian populations, led to unprecedented damage to life and, of course, property. Like so many other groups, companies and communities M&B faced the challenge of rebuilding. The chairman of M&B, Arthur Mitchell, seemed to echo earlier company policy when he suggested that the rebuilding required would lead to a condition where there were 'no redundant or badly constructed licensed houses in the country'. The returning service people and their civilian counterparts were ready for change as the prompt removal of Churchill in the 1945 election illustrated.

Despite these difficulties, Cape Hill and M&B were to enjoy remarkable success in this post-war period. The board continued the pre-war policy of 'fewer and better' pubs which seemed in tune with people's aspirations, and by the end of 1945 Cape Hill had increased its production to 963,000 barrels a year. Through the lean late 1940s progress was steadily maintained and by 1949 the estate of M&B consisted of 873 tied pubs, 14 tenanted houses, 86 managed houses and a further 358 off-licences. Cape Hill was delivering over 70% of its production to tied houses, an enviable position in 1949, but before long these so-called monopolies were to exercise the mind of government. By 1955 there was the first evidence of changing tastes: M&B alone was selling over £2,000,000s worth of wines and spirits annually while beer barrel production had eased to 794,000, some 18% down on their figures of 10 years earlier.

# GOOD HONEST BEER

That M&B was still a cash-rich company can be seen from reports regarding their building programmes. In 1947 Robert Butler reported that the company had spent £5,000,000 on building alone since 1920 but only the two share issues of 1928 and 1938 (which realized around 25%) had actually been required. The ambitious redevelopment by Birmingham Corporation led M&B to earmark the rebuilding of 170 houses purely as a result of the inner ring road. At this stage the company was not envisaging growth in beer sales, at least not in Birmingham itself. In 1953 Robert Butler addressed the AGM thus:

'Brewers in Birmingham can in total only expect the same amount of trade from the city unless, of course, there should be a marked increase in the consumption of beer per head - which seems unlikely'.

This stagnation led the company to look farther afield for business opportunities and, for the first time, M&B became a 'player' in South Wales. In 1950 they acquired Thatcher's Brewery of Newport and with it a small tied house estate. M&BG (South Wales) Ltd was the result and the following year they acquired 95 more tied houses when they bought out Darby's Brewery in West Bromwich. This was a takeover based on a family friendship: the Darby family was facing heavy estate duty payments and friendship with Robert Butler facilitated a satisfactory piece of business for all concerned. Darby's Bitter continued to be brewed for a while, although at Cape Hill, while all the tied houses were supplied and stocked by M&B.

It is about this time that the business ethos of M&B began to change. In order to remain independent growth was required, and growth required cash, lots of it. Share issues raised money but the company's considerable reserves were inevitably reduced. Despite some reluctance within the company to go down this road it is apparent that M&B remained a huge operating company. Even allowing for depreciation in the value of money, the company's reserve of £350,000 in 1920 had risen to £3,300,000 in 1948 and rose to £6,233,640 over the following decade. During most of the 1950s, some 60% of gross profit was going in taxation and margins were squeezed. In 1951 M&B reported that net profits were 2.7%. The directly managed estate kept costs tight but in the property booms of the years to come these tied houses were not realizing their potential purely as bricks and mortar.

In 1955 the Cheltenham and Hereford Breweries Ltd was targeted by a well-financed property speculation grouping and only kept their company intact by surrendering a large chunk of their business to Whitbread. Whitbread's chairman, while happy to expand his company, reported to his shareholders that 'a company which has run its finances in the most conservative manner, ploughing back a large portion of its profits into the business, may lay itself open to FINANCIAL MARAUDERS WHO PLAN TO TAKE IT OVER, LIQUIDATE IT, AND SELL ITS ASSETS…' The brewers had been put on notice and by one of their own. Four years later a bid by Sears Holdings for Watney Mann, although ultimately a failure, further concentrated the mind.

Brewers understood that their tied house system, while guaranteeing sales for their products, needed to be rationalized in order to realize their true worth. Small concerns with small estates were, reasonably enough, keen to hold on to their precarious market share, but say you had 150 tied houses and you merged with a company who likewise had 150 tied houses, you could have 225 houses in which to sell your products and 75 properties to sell. Given that you were probably already competing for the same market share with over half your original estate, the case for merging became compelling. And, of course, if you owned over 1,000 tied houses…

M&B were not removed from this changing climate. In 1956 the company's merchant banker, Helbert Wagg & Co, had become concerned at what they perceived to be in-fighting between the 'family' directors and, knowing that some retirements were due, insisted on the appointment of a new chief executive director who should be neither a Mitchell nor a Butler - Alan Walker. His career to date had been largely spent within the sugar industry, much of it abroad. A non-brewery man, he met the banker's desire to appoint somebody 'with wide commercial experience'.

Alan Walker's appointment led to considerable change at M&B. The previous year had seen some talks between them and Ansells but apart from an agreement over building programmes in Birmingham, which led to the 1957 formation of Associated Midland Brewers Ltd, these came to nothing. After a short review, Walker decided that the company was over-manned, sales were relatively stagnant and that the large cash reserves were just not being robustly used. Within three years he achieved, as planned, a 30% increase in sales and reduced the workforce by nearly 800. He also reintroduced the virtual non-stop use of all capital equipment which surely would have chimed well with Henry Mitchell during his early brewing days in Smethwick. He also changed the emphasis within the company whereby the brewing staff seemed to enjoy higher status than the sales and marketing employees. As a non-brewery man, he bravely instructed that the draught mild be strengthened and enjoyed the subsequent rise in sales. He was also responsible for the re-naming of the company bitter as 'Brew X1', a great latter day M&B success story.

Further developments saw sales in the free trade sector rise from 17% of turnover to 30% in three years and Walker restarted the company's acquisition programme. Atkinson's Brewery Ltd with a brewery in Aston and 360 tied houses was acquired in 1959. The Horton family, who were the major equity owner in the company, had family connections with the Butlers (William Waters's daughter, Edna, had married Victor Horton) and were bought out on good terms, although the apparent guarantee that the brewery would stay open, with its weekly production of 3,000 barrels, did not happen. In the same year, M&B acquired W. Butler & Co. Ltd of Wolverhampton. Of no family connection, this concern owned 830 licensed premises including a considerable presence in Shrewsbury. Referring back to 1955, and Col. Whitbread's warnings, this acquisition seems to have been most friendly as the Wolverhampton company had no desire to be swallowed by a non-brewery concern.

We have seen that Davenports in Birmingham built up a substantial home delivery business around this time. Drinking at home and the rapid expansion of other leisure activities were combining to pressurize the brewing industry, making it even more important to provide pleasant surrounding for their customers. As early as 1952 in an article entitled 'Economic Trends in the Brewing Industry' The Statist presciently suggested that 'brewers who have traditionally regarded themselves as brewers first and last may have to consider themselves increasingly as owners of property'. In Birmingham where M&B managed (in 1949) 86% of their houses and Ansells some 80%, it seems that this suggestion had been acted upon but it was the very act of the monopoly this created that sowed the seeds of their eventual fall.

In a very short period from 1955 there was a merging of many small brewers, medium size ones and much larger enterprises, all of which created an atmosphere of 'monopoly'. In 1955 there were 10 brewery mergers, followed by 19 in 1956, 10 in 1957, 10 in 1958, 22 in 1959 and 28 alone in 1960. These 99 mergers in a mere five-year period were followed by 21 in 1961, 13 in 1962, 7 in 1964, 9 in 1965 and 6 in 1966, with a further 60 over the next 5 years, and by 1971 a further 29 mergers had taken place. While many of these mergers involved the coming together or takeover of modest companies, it is during this period that the so called 'Big Six' appeared. By 1967 there was an inquiry by the Monopolies Commission into Allied, Bass Charrington (this company just formed from a merger of them both), Guinness, Scottish & Newcastle, Watney, and Whitbread.

The remarkable performance of M&B under Alan Walker after 1956 strengthened their position in the industry but success always attracts suitors and M&B was anxious to build a national presence on top of its regional prowess. Bass, Ratcliff and Gretton Ltd attracted Walker's attention twofold. They owned two household names,

Worthington and Bass, and their network was truly national, their beers selling from the southwest to the northeast and in all the major conurbations of the UK. With over £8,000,000 in reserve, this was a truly massive company but, like M&B before 1956, had to some extent stood still. Essentially a free trade company, the amalgamation with the tied house estate of M&B made good sense. Bass Mitchells & Butlers became a reality in July 1961, a coming together unimaginable only a few years earlier, but Bass was in long term decline while M&B, at that time, was a company on the up.

The first period in the new company's life was not easy. Entrenched boardroom practices at Bass led Walker to keep a low profile until becoming chairman late in 1963. He immediately introduced a programme of staff reductions while improving pay at junior levels. Looking to further the company, Walker was no longer interested in small regional acquisitions but was eager to expand a national enterprise. After a fierce competitive struggle with Watney Mann, Bass M&B landed the considerable fish that was Bent Brewery Co. Ltd who had considerable holdings in and around Liverpool, totalling some 500 houses. Beer barrelage in Liverpool was high although many of the pubs were very basic. One wonders what William Waters Butler would have made of the following description of the drinking environment: 'conditions and expectations were very different on Merseyside. In many pubs the most important member of the bar staff was the Alsatian'.

In June 1967 a merger between Charrington United Breweries and Bass M&B became a reality after the respective chairmen first discussed the proposal while standing in the slips during a brewery cricket match.

These mergers led to yet more government inquiries and reports. Four reports in 1966, 1969 (2) and 1977 were all critical of these large companies and their perceived overpricing which it was believed was a direct result of their monopoly. In fact rising beer prices were below the national retail price index in every year from 1953 to 1978, and twice, in 1978 and 1979, applications to raise beer prices by Allied and Whitbread were authorized by the Price Commission. At the same time some reserve was expressed about an increase that Bass was seeking. In other words, the brewers were pushing their boundaries, looking to expand but not exploiting their customer base. The author remembers ordering a Light & Bitter in London one hot day in London in 1978. The price in Surrey for the same Courage drink came to 28p and, when asked for 38p, I decided to remain hot!

The Bass M&B merger with Charrington in 1967 saw the estate expand to over 10,000 tied premises. Perhaps it is this merger that, ironically, sowed the first seeds of Cape Hill's eventual demise as they were now just one of a national network of breweries as opposed to a kingpin one. The year 1982 saw the closure of Ansells and the end of a century long competition for business in Birmingham. Despite the opportunity provided by this vast gap in the market, it now became the era of rapidly diminishing staff levels at Cape Hill as brewers needed far fewer people to meet the demand for keg beer which was rapidly overtaking that of cask beer, this despite the success of organisations like CAMRA who looked to keep the flag for 'real ale' flying. In 1977 Cape Hill was still producing a mighty 2,197,000 barrels a year. Ten years later this had fallen to 1,730,000.

Modernization and changing demands for beer led the company to decide on the demolition of Henry Mitchell's original No 1 Brewery. Work started in 1985 but a major fire, on the 17th July 1986, delayed this project, which was eventually completed in 1987. The fire vindicated Henry Mitchell's original decision to keep the two breweries apart as production in No 2 Brewery was not seriously affected.

GOOD HONEST BEER

SPORT & LEISURE

M&B had a long tradition of looking after its staff which is reflected by the usually good industrial relations that existed at Cape Hill. Obviously there were tensions from time to time (as we saw with wages in an earlier chapter).

At the beginning of the company's life in 1898, a pension scheme was set up, all funds being contributed by the company. Pensions were to be awarded as reward for long service (20 years). This was followed in 1901 by a form of medical insurance, again funded by the company.

The fine facilities provided by the company gave many employees the chance to shine at sport.

In 1954 the cricket teams won both divisions of The Birmingham and District League and Alan Townsend became, in 1961, the first player in the league's history to score 1,000 league runs in a season and, for good measure, he repeated this success in 1970. The fine cricket ground at the rear of the brewery hosted top quality matches throughout its life. In 1931 Warwickshire played a first class fixture versus Kent there and the ground was used nine times for county fixtures before the war. Although 1st X1 county fixtures were rare after 1945 (it was used in 1957) the county 2nd XI played many fixtures there until 1992 and The International Cricket Conference used the facility on a regular basis.

Happily the ground was used for less serious encounters from time to time. The company magazine, The Deerstalker, records a fixture on the 12th May 1949 when a Brewery X1 narrowly defeated The Brewing School in a 20 over evening game. As the report dwelt evenly on the snooker, sandwiches and beer taken after the match, it is fair to suggest that this was a social occasion.

159

GOOD HONEST BEER

A boxing club was opened in 1946, joining the bowling club (1920) and both the tennis and table tennis clubs represented the company in local leagues as well as organizing their own 'in house' competitions. Fishing was popular and there were gardening, golf and photography groups all adding to the choice of leisure activities available.

Harry Butler, brother of William Waters, was a keen amateur athletics fan and the superb running track and facilities were often made available for local schools to use for their sports days. As well as giving children an opportunity to compete in excellent conditions, the company was opening its doors to prospective new employees.

In 2010 I was invited to the M&B social club on Portland Road. Originally opened on the 1$^{st}$ May 1950, it stands amongst houses bought and built for company employees and the outline of the brewery is still just about recognizable through the trees while the rear of the Pumping Station is clearly visible. On a 2010 website I noted that the club was a venue for salsa dancing evenings: strictly of course!

## CHAPTER 12: THE BEER ORDERS 1989 AND A NEW ORDER

Along with many of their competitors, Bass M&B had spent a decade and a great deal of money improving their sites and positioning themselves for the undoubted challenges ahead. But nothing had prepared them for the results of an inquiry into monopolies by the Competition Commission which reported in 1989.

Legislation which followed, The Supply of Beer (Tied Estate) Order 1989 and The Supply of Beer (Loan Ties, Licensed Premises & Wholesale Prices) Order 1989 completely altered the face of the industry and led directly to the destruction of so much that the likes of Henry Mitchell and William Butler had created.

Reviewed just over a decade later, the Beer Orders, as these two acts became known, were revoked in their entirety in 2003, but the dramatic changes they invoked had gone too far and the inquiries and legislation that followed led directly to the demise of Cape Hill and other breweries.

The report itself is very long and exhaustive and can be accessed on the internet, but it is worth looking at the summary. Some readers may feel that its inclusion is unnecessary but I believe it is an integral part of the story of Cape Hill's last days. I have edited many sentences and paragraphs, but the words reproduced are as per the report.

Readers today can consider the power of just a few supermarket companies who, it seems, have a position in the market far more dominant and pervasive than the target of this report.

The Supply of Beer: A report on the supply of beer for retail sale in the United Kingdom.

Summary

Our terms of reference require us to investigate and report on whether a monopoly situation exists in relation to the supply of beer for retail sale in the United Kingdom. We have unanimously concluded that a monopoly exists in favour of those brewers who own tied houses or who have tying agreements with free houses in return for loans at favourable interest rates.

Although our terms of reference are prescribed by United Kingdom law, nevertheless the law of the European Community has formed, throughout our enquiry, an additional and important element in our deliberations. In particular we have taken into account Commission Regulation 1984/83, which contains a block exemption for certain beer supply agreements. This block exemption is qualified and of finite duration. Its existence does not prevent us from recommending changes.

Author's Note: So from the start we can see that the policy that Henry Mitchell and William Butler had followed in the building of their enterprise is no longer acceptable and that powers invested from far away could be used to eventually destroy a business in a community in which it neither had contact nor any interest. The summary continues:

Although sales of beer in off-licences and supermarkets are growing, 85 per cent of beer is consumed in public houses, clubs and other on-licensed premises. The public house remains central to the nation's beer-drinking habits.

# GOOD HONEST BEER

Premises serving alcohol in the United Kingdom require a licence. In 1986 there were some 192,000 licences in issue, nearly 40% more than in 1966. Since a public house requires a full on-licence, it follows that the increase in the number of public houses over the last 20 years has been low.

---

Author's Note: A public house has to be an orderly house, something a responsible brewer and tenant are expected to run and be held responsible for in law, while cheap drink bought in supermarkets just cannot be so monitored, even if the will exists to do so.

---

Brewing companies differ greatly in size, but the majority of them brew beer AND wholesale it AND retail it. We estimate that brewers own about 75% of the public house in Great Britain managed and tied.
We identified over 200 brewers. 6 National brewers account for 75% of beer production, 74% of the brewer-owned estate and 86% of loan ties, 11 regional brewers, 41 local brewers, 3 brewers without tied estate (Carlsberg, Guinness and Northern Clubs Federation) and 160 other brewers, all operating on a very small scale.

Throughout our inquiry we were struck by the vigour and thoroughness of The Brewer's Society response to the many questions we asked and the points we put back to it. There is no doubt in our minds that the Society is formidably effective in championing its members' interests.

---

Author's Note: The incredulity at somebody not only making something but selling it as well is a good illustration of why so much of our manufacturing base has been allowed to wither. No wonder the breweries defended themselves with such 'vigour'. This summary has been heavily edited but the final view and recommendations of the

163

Commission are laid out more fully. Let the Commission speak for itself:

---

Our View

Eloquently though the industry's case has been put, we are not persuaded that all is well. We have confirmed our provisional finding that a complex monopoly situation exists in favour of the brewers with tied estates and loan ties.

This complex monopoly restricts competition at all levels. Brewers are protected from competition in supplying their managed and tenanted estates because other brewers do not have access to them. Even in the free trade many brewers prefer to compete by offering low-interest loans, which then tie the outlet to them, rather than by offering beer at lower prices. Wholesale prices are higher than they would be in the absence of the tie. This inevitably feeds through into high retail prices.

The ownership and loan ties also give little opportunity for an independent wholesaling sector to prosper and offer competition to the brewer's wholesaling activities, for example by offering a mix of products from different producers.

At the retail level the effect of the high wholesale price is that free houses cannot offer effective competition to the brewers' own managed and tenanted outlets. Because wholesale prices are too high, there is pressure on the free trade to accept loans, which then fetter their ability to attract customers by offering their own distinctive range of products, drawn from many brewers. The development of independent retail chains of the sort seen in the off-licensed trade is also heavily restricted. Although the brewers have been investing heavily in their public houses, and use this as a justification for higher prices, there is no opportunity for these developments to be tested by competition to whether consumers are getting the mixture of price and amenity that they really want.

In summary, we believe that the monopoly has enabled brewers with tied estates to frustrate the growth of brewers without tied estates;

We believe that structural changes are essential to source a more competitive regime which will in turn remedy the detriments.

Our Recommendations

The Property Tie

It has been put to us repeatedly that smaller brewers in particular need their tied estates to stay in business. In present circumstances, if the tie were to be abolished altogether we believe that many regional and local brewers would withdraw from brewing, concentrate on retailing, and leave the market to domination by national and international brand owners. This would be substantially reduce consumer choice. We therefore recommend, not the complete abolition of the tie, but a ceiling of 2,000 on the number of on-licensed premises, whether public houses, hotels or any other type of on-licensed outlet. This ceiling will require the divestment of some 22,000 premises by national brewers. We do not believe that property or capital markets will have any difficulty in absorbing the change.

The Loan Tie

We recommend the elimination of all loan ties.

The Product Tie

We recommend that a tenant should be allowed to purchase a minimum of one brand of draught beer from a supplier other than his landlord.

GOOD HONEST BEER

Author's Note: Certainly the Product Tie recommendation seems eminently reasonable but the contemporary reader can only wonder how the boards of today's supermarkets would react to the recommendations on outlet numbers. There was monopoly and, as we have seen, many earlier governments and local authorities preferred to work with fewer, larger, better run companies.

The report is an exhaustive piece of work covering all aspects of the brewing industry. For the purposes of this work and because of the way in which Henry Mitchell and William Butler nurtured their business, I place most emphasis on those areas of the report dealing with tied houses. The report had 164 paragraphs of conclusion and was signed by the chairman R G Smethurst and four colleagues, but there was a note of dissent from L A Mills running to 58 paragraphs, including a quote in Greek from Aristotle. He agreed that a 'complex monopoly exists in the United Kingdom brewing industry' but:

Para 3 'Where I do not agree that public interest detriments arise – but my colleagues find they do arise – I consider that the recommendations are unnecessary and indeed could lead to a reduction of competition and consumer choice'.

Para 14 '...I find that the major recommendation to limit the number of Public Houses owned by the brewers and to abolish the loan tie are, in my view, neither desirable nor necessary'.

Para 15 'the limitation of ownership of 2,000 public houses by each brewer means that some 22,000 public houses currently owned by brewers – with an estimated value of several billion pounds – would have to be sold. The presumption behind this divestment is that the public houses will be bought and used as public houses by others in a more competitive situation. However, what is highly doubtful in my view is whether they would in fact ALL be bought and – even if they were – whether they would continue to be used as public houses'.

The Commission found that the Big Six had estates of 33,900 pubs and thus were expecting them to sell 21,900. Bass itself was required to sell off 5,300 premises, thus reducing the market for its own brewed products considerably. The average price of a pint in 1989, when this report turned into law, was £1.08. In the following 20 years, after both the Beer Orders and the monopoly rulings of the Blair administrations, the average price had leapt to £2.81 and is still rising fast. On the 11th August 2010, the British Beer & Pub Association was warning of a £4 pint and noted that increases in beer duty over the past two years had been a staggering 26% (see Sir William's letter of 1931).

The legislation arising from the Beer Orders came into law in 1990. By 2000 the estates of the big brewers had dwindled from an overall pub ownership of 53% in the United Kingdom to under 15%. Government returned to the legislation in 2000 and again in April 2002 when my then local MP, Richard Younger-Ross, secured a debate on revoking the beer orders. The situation of the small brewer as opposed to the big one was still a vexed issue. The orders were revoked in January 2003 and just over two years later CAMRA was complaining that takeovers by Greene King and Wolverhampton & Dudley respectively were giving them estates of over 2,000 pubs each, the very thing the Beer Orders were supposed to prevent.

Whether the Beer Orders were a force for good or bad remains debateable, but they were certainly contentious. The dissent of L A Mills in 1989, according to Martin Thomas whose brewery career included appointments at Cape Hill:

'reflected the views of many in the industry that the proposals would have a negative effect'. He continued: 'The striking loss for me was the removal of the long-term investment in pub assets and licensee training exercised by the big brewers for their tenancies. The emerging pub companies of the 1990s were built on debt and short-term financial targets. This has caused real stress during the recent financial crisis but many tenants or leaseholders today have seen all incentive evaporate (squeezed by very high rents and high prices for beer charged to them by the pub companies themselves, not by brewers). The major brewers tried hard to support tenants and also permitted guest ales so I'm not sure what has been gained from so much disruption and the future of many community pubs particularly has been lost or put at risk'.

In 1989 the Big Six between them owned 34,059 pubs. Following the Beer Orders and the selling off of pubs it was assumed that the picture would radically change. In fact, by 2004, 10 companies still owned 29,281 of which 25,906 were owned by the six biggest. Over 80% of all beer sold in Great Britain was brewed by SIX companies. No wonder that the orders were repealed as 'pointless legislation'.

In 1989 a pint of beer cost 96p, a pint of lager £1.08. At the start of the 1997 Labour administration, these figures were £1.63 and £1.81, rising to £2.39 and £2.74 by 2008.

In 2003 came 24-hour drinking, recession and closures. In 2007 alone 1,409 pubs closed. By March 2008 a staggering 27 were closing each week, this figure rising to 52 by July 2009. By September 2010 the National Housing Federation was lamenting that village life was 'dying out', highlighting the closures of pubs, shops and schools.

Considering Wellington's Beer Act of 1830, the endless legislation of those restless Victorians, the spiteful interfering of Lloyd George and the reports from various monopoly commissions, the story of brewery legislation is one of unremitting muddle, interference and, in the final analysis, failure. At least Lloyd George enrolled brewers onto the Carlisle committee. But the later Beer Orders and the Labour Licensing Acts could never be called successful.

Finally, the realignment in the industry after the Beer Orders legislation led The Brewers Society, formed in 1904, and which fought so tenaciously against Lloyd George's vindictive 1908 proposals, to rename itself The Brewers and Licensed Retailers Association. In 1995 non-UK brewers were welcomed as members.

## CHAPTER 13: A VIEW FROM THE INSIDE & THE OUTSIDE

Following the Beer Orders legislation of 1990 and the subsequent years of rejigging, Bass made two attempts to reposition themselves in a rapidly-expanding global business. In 1997 they proposed a merger with Carlsberg-Tetley but Margaret Beckett, minister at the DTI, ruled it as being against the public interest, the same fate as befell the proposed 2000 merger with Interbrew. This time the ruling was given by Stephen Byers.

Following these two reversals it seems that the writing was on the wall for Cape Hill. Helping me understand the gradual decline, I was fortunate enough to meet Martin Thomas (see also page 167) at the Armistice Service in November 2010. I understood at this chance meeting that Martin had worked at Cape Hill in several managerial roles and we chatted along with two of his former colleagues. I contacted Martin a few weeks later and we started a correspondence that resulted in much that follows. While I have sourced information from Martin, any opinions expressed and any errors made are mine. The following observations, printed below, were sent to me by Martin in December 2010 and February 2011 and are reproduced in an edited form with his permission. I hope they will give the reader a real glimpse of what it was like working inside the brewery:

---

'Cape Hill is where I was interviewed for a job in 1976 and my first "home" brewery. The whole site just oozed tradition, scale and excitement for a young "would be" brewer. The brewery was one of the big 4 in the 13 brewery Bass network at that time, producing a lot of keg and cask beer especially in those famous Midlands brands, Brew X1 and M&B Mild. I can remember the traditional hierarchy illustrated by at least three levels of restaurant! The directors had theirs in those imposing offices on Cape Hill and the brewers even had their own oak panelled room in the brewery (the one that burned down) which served amazing breakfasts for the brewers on early shift.

# GOOD HONEST BEER

I left all this behind in 1977 when I was packed off to Yorkshire but was thrilled to return as Brewery Director in 1989. My memories of working at Cape Hill are a wonderful mix of the very traditional wooden and copper brewhouse which reminded me of being aboard a grand old ship in some ways with the narrow stairs and big structures. Also very traditional were the extensive fermenting rooms in that enormous brick building that could have stood for 1,000 years...and the cask racking area, so evocative of all that is magical about traditional beers with the large barrels, the smells, the swinging of the mallets as the shives were driven home. Big guys in aprons amongst the steam, hops and noise...

In contrast, in later years there were the modern process areas at the other end of the manufacturing and technology spectrum. Shiny stainless steel, automatic valves, computer control and very few people to operate such areas, high speed bottling and canning equipment, food factory hygiene standards and more computer wizardry It was the blending of the heritage with the contemporary that made Cape Hill a fascinating brewery to work in during those final years...

In truth, at that time industrial relations were not good (a legacy shared by all large breweries whose management had grown used to giving in to most demands in order to keep the beer flowing during the good times). I recall my task as trying to gain some control and a shared agenda with the T&G Union and believe I established a sensible working relationship with the convenor and his shop stewards. This was important in order to attract investment. (Beer volumes were now contracting and the breweries in the Bass group competed with each other for cash.) We were able to position Cape as worthy of significant investment which became known as Cape 94, a £60m plus investment in 2 bottling lines and a canning line completed in 94. (I was appointed to Britvic as Operations Director in late 1991.)

This investment saw export volumes concentrated at Cape during the mid-nineties and with draught volumes falling, the 750,000 barrels of

Export Bass (mostly for the USA) became the lifeblood of the brewery. You could buy Export Bass from Cape in every state in the US. These developments were ironically sowing the seeds of the eventual downfall of the brewery. I returned to Bass Brewers in 1996 as Group Production Director and sadly in many ways was obliged to oversee a consolidation programme in the late nineties closing Sheffield and Cardiff ale breweries but also our neighbouring lager brewery to increase the size of Burton. Cape meanwhile was secure with the export work.

In 1999, Bass Plc. announced that the brewing division would be sold and that the hotel and pub business would be renamed Six Continents. In August 2000 the sale was agreed to Interbrew amid much excitement, here was a beer company going places. We were soon facing the disappointment of a competition inquiry in the UK as Interbrew had also purchased the Whitbread beer business a few months earlier. After 10 long months, in June 2001, the DTI announced that the merger with Interbrew was to be prohibited. After a long drawn out legal challenge, the England and Wales portion of Bass Brewers was put up for sale (again). Interbrew argued successfully that there were no competition issues in Scotland or Ireland, nor were there issues outside the UK. This led to Interbrew keeping the two breweries in Glasgow and Belfast, keeping the Bass name and the overseas business in Czech Republic and the export volume. Crucially, however, they said they would brew the latter in a former Whitbread brewery (Salmesbury) and would not keep Cape Hill despite a high level of recent investment in all areas and a good performance. This effectively sounded the death knell of the brewery. It was one of the saddest decisions I ever faced and yet one of the most compelling. Short of closing Burton (and the numbers didn't add up), Cape had to be sold or run down; it was about to be a brewery with nothing to brew. Though we tried there were no takers for a sale and we had a year's contract to supply Interbrew and make our closure plans.

The whole team of 300 or so at Cape were magnificent that last year (effectively calendar 2003, the second sale to Coors was agreed close to Christmas Eve 2001 and sealed $2^{nd}$ Feb 2002). The team pulled together with tremendous energy and dignity. They were determined to go out on a high and they did, with some of the best performance figures ever. (I have seen this a few times, a kind of "adversity spirit" kicks in and people pull together almost like never before.) The management team worked hard getting jobs and providing support, many guys went on to fulfilling careers elsewhere. Redundancy terms were generous. We got down to a handful who were neither fixed up nor happy to retire.

The parallel activity in 2003 was selling the site and for good or bad the major interest came from the house builders and that brings us up to date'.

---

The house builders were Persimmon. They agreed to purchase the 78 acre site, paying £6,000,000 in 2004 followed by a further £20,000,000 the following year. I have come across some fairly silly and vitriolic postings on the internet about the redevelopment. It is hardly surprising that rats were found in the maze of cellars and old buildings. Clearing and filling in the site must have been a considerable task. A comprehensive environmental study was made of the area and the whole development, still unfinished (2011) is certainly very smart. They have used the names attached to the brewery as part of their strategy and Mitchells Brook and Deer Leap are two of these.

Industrial relations were obviously difficult during these last years. Generally the paternal nature of the brewery companies, the attention to the welfare of their staff and, presumably, acceptable rates of pay, made the brewing industry one of the more stable areas of the economy. Union recognition came relatively late, the TGWU first being mentioned in M&B minutes in 1938. After the war, and with a sympathetic Labour government, the TGWU lobbied hard for national working conditions, standardizing wages and hours. By the nature of the small specialist groups of workers required in a brewery this was resisted by the brewers but, gradually, labour costs became subject to national agreements. Not surprisingly, the massive mergers of the 1960s alarmed both workforces and their union representatives and, as companies became more and more part of a national enterprise, it inevitably led to these agreements.

No company is perfect. The undoubted monopoly that M&B had in certain areas of the Midlands did lead to an element of complacency. The story below, for which I thank O C Darby, ex-chairman of M&B, is a classic.

One warm afternoon, the chairman, after a quick round of golf, decided to call in at The Abbey, a large M&B pub, for a half of mild. Situated on Abbey Road, the pub was less than a mile from Cape Hill. The only other customers were three men, nursing three pints of mild. Apparently they decided their beer was cloudy and asked for a change; on being told there was nothing wrong with their beer they decided to leave. The chairman noted that his glass of mild was indeed cloudy and politely suggested to the publican that he too would like his drink changed only to be met by a torrent of abuse and a suggestion that he went forth and so on…

Apparently by dinner time the following day, not one brewery employee was unaware of the chairman's dissatisfaction. The Abbey is still trading today, although one suspects there may have been a change in personnel!

Until the redevelopments of the 1960s, there was a row of terraced properties opposite the brewery, running down Cape Hill, past the junction with Raglan Road and down to the crossroads at the bottom of the hill. Several of these housed small businesses that, to an extent, relied on M&B and its workforce for their livelihoods.

# GOOD HONEST BEER

In the years immediately after the 1939-45 war there were two grocery shops, one run by the Misses Savage on Raglan Road, the other on Cape Hill run by Mrs Kelsey. Previously a cook, Mrs Kelsey provided a basic hot food takeaway service, her stew and fish and chips being the mainstays. Pam McCarron, born in 1947, remembers these shops, the newsagent where she collected her weekly comic and a café where they served 'the most fantastic bacon or sausage sandwiches. In the school holidays there was nothing more I enjoyed than going to the café and collecting hot sandwiches for our mid-day meal. It was full of people from the brewery who had come over for something to eat'.

In 1947, Pam's grandfather opened a shop as an electrical contractor, E. Minchin & Son. He took in repair work, recharged batteries, sold new appliances and, as his main business, built up a steady relationship with the brewery who engaged him for call outs both at the brewery and many of their pubs and depots.

Pam's father was a good friend of Ken Fisher, elder brother of Vernon who has been such a great help with my researches into M&B and especially the Cape Hill Fire Brigade (starting on page 62). Many houses around Cape Hill were owned by M&B and it was company policy to house their firemen in proximity to the brewery, making it easier and quicker if a 'turn out' was required.

No 161 Cape Hill belonged to the brewery and a lady who lived there, Mrs Blanchett, was a M&B personnel officer, responsible for the hiring of female staff. Apart from her work, this lady was well-known locally for her cooking. She made pastry for pies and tarts (using all butter), made pies for friends and baked for her neighbours at Christmas. At her retirement she moved to London to be with her son and the house was made available to another family of firemen, the Woodrows.

Inside the brewery itself there were so many different functions necessary for the smooth running of the business. Returning to the

1931 map, one realizes that apart from brewing staff, draymen, coopers, bottlers, chemists, clerks and the odd chairman, there were also stabling staff, garage mechanics, canteen staff and so on. It must have taken a considerable amount of company time keeping the yards brushed and tidy. One chairman was noted for the example he set as he brushed the area outside his office each and every morning before starting work.

Sue Timmins, who now lives in Dover, was responsible during her time at M&B for sorting out the insurance on all the company cars used by the reps and for the claims that the inevitable bumps and scrapes would have caused.

These few vignettes only offer a glimpse of the activity and community around The Cape Hill Brewery. It is more than a century since Henry Mitchell opened his brewery and it is intriguing to wonder what the locality will look like in another hundred years.

CHAPTER 14: MITCHELLS & BUTLERS PLC AND INTO THE 21$^{ST}$ CENTURY

The website of the new M&B informs us that the Beer Orders changed everything. Before looking at the new company it is interesting to see what an older brewer made of the changes during his career. Sydney Nevile entered the trade in 1890 and served with William Waters Butler on The LCCB. In 1958, looking back on his career he noted that beer was much stronger when he started and the amount of beer brewed had dropped dramatically from its heyday in 1914. Nevile's view of the 'tied' house was:

---

In 1890 the ownership of public houses by brewers was growing rapidly and was developing in two directions. On the one hand, as public houses came into the market they were bought up by brewers to secure a regular output for their beers. On the other hand, in many parts of the country (notably in the Midlands and Lancashire), prosperous publicans who had acquired a number of houses purchased a brewery in order to supply their needs, continuing their retail business through managers. It is incorrect to designate such concerns as 'tied houses' - they are no more 'tied' than are the distributive branches of such multiple firms as Boots, the chemists...'

---

When Bass decided to sell off its brewery arm to Interbrew, they had committed themselves to their hotel division. As part of this change of emphasis, and because they had also sold the old company name, they renamed themselves Six Continents Plc. Happily this dreary corporate name was short-lived. Early in 2001 the company sold 988 pubs to Japan's Nomura group for £625,000,000 with a view to expanding the hotel division. Less than two years later, with a falling share price and rumblings from shareholders, the company split itself into two. The hotel business was to be called the Intercontinental Hotels Group which left them with an unnamed pub and restaurant division.

# GOOD HONEST BEER

Perhaps still reeling from the lack of identity that the name Six Continents had given the pubs, a decision was made to re-link with the past, and a new division launched itself on the London Stock Exchange in April 2003 with the familiar name: Mitchells & Butlers.

Mitchells & Butlers has its head office in Fleet Street, Birmingham. According to recent accounts M&B employs over 38,000 people, and has over 2,000 pubs and restaurants. There is no brewery activity at all, everything being sourced from outside. Obviously this is a very considerable company but it has not been easy going since its inception. An interview with new Chairman John Lovering in September 2010 in The Daily Telegraph mentioned a 'group that has undue notoriety in recent years after shareholder spats, executive departures and eye-watering losses'. This included a massive loss of £500,000,000 in a failed 2007 property joint venture. Indeed Lovering's appointment itself seems to have been contentious: The Daily Telegraph headline, covering the story on 29th January 2010 reported:

John Lovering named new M&B chair after bar brawl.

Another pretty scathing observation, made in The Spectator on the 23rd January 2010, spoke of a one-time respected brewery being one that 'these days symbolizes everything that's depressing about modern corporate wheeler-dealing'. After a 60-day review of the company by John Lovering and the new board, a chunk of pubs, bowling alleys and small hotels were sold off, assets worth £500,000,000. And yet, barely four months later, on the 24th January 2011, Lovering announced he was standing down amid hints that he and major shareholders were not seeing eye to eye.

Whatever the rights and wrongs, and with the different pressures of business today, it can be seen that the new M&B is far removed from its ancestors. Turning over vast amounts of money, it does not strike the note of consistent, well managed growth that existed under the old Cape Hill/M&B.

I visited the Fleet Street office in April 2010 and was made welcome. The building is modern, working conditions seem excellent and yet it is a puzzle that there are manifestly considerable problems. Could it be that the company seems to be run from afar (one group of speculators have been named the Sandy Lane Set based in Barbados) and that there is no strong control on the ground. Certainly, as one journalist put it, it's all run 'a long way from Smethwick'.

During the 1950s we saw that brewers became more sensitive to the value of their property portfolios and strove to achieve a balance with their brewing activities. After 1989 and The Beer Orders it seems that the ownership of property, of pubs, became more important still until, finally, the ownership of a pub itself completely took over from the original reason for buying it which was to supply it with beer.

CHAPTER 15: CONCLUSION

'Recession and property slump signals last orders for 250-strong pub chain'

'Coalition to curb 24-hour drinking'

'A record number of outlets sell alcohol'

'Demonising a few drinks with friends is the fear'

'Chairman can't resist the lure of a pub challenge'

These are just a few headlines collected over the past couple of years which indicate that all was not well within the brewing industry, yet there are still people and companies willing to try and make a living from it today.

This story started with The Beer Act of 1830 and during the next 180 years there has been this continual conflict between government, vested interests, monopolies and the perceived 'public good'. More than anything there seems to be a mistrust of any organization capable of not only making their product but having the temerity to market it via their own auspices. We now have an economy wherein, according to the last quarter's 2010 figures, just 13% of it is in manufacturing. (Interestingly this was the only sector showing growth.)

Birmingham rose to become an industrial giant, yet by the 12$^{th}$ October 2009 a Daily Telegraph article written by Graham Ruddick reported under the headline, 'Birmingham seeks Middle East cash':

'Much-maligned manufacturing heartland of Britain seeks exotic cash-rich partner from Middle East. That's the message being put forward by Birmingham as it fights to overcome the recession. The UK's second city has turned to the Middle East in a desperate attempt to kick-start major property developments that have been halted because of the financial crisis…starting developments is key to the economic recovery of the UK's second city, where unemployment is among the highest in the country…particular developments…the £150m V-tower, Ballymore's 350,000 sq. ft. residential and five-star hotel scheme…'

Building hotels and office blocks employs many people, but for how long? Any visitor to Birmingham today will observe towers and blocks lying empty while the manufacturing base has almost completely disappeared. The Ordnance Survey maps of the early 20th century illustrate just how much has been lost. On the 1901 Smethwick sheet, Grove Lane opposite Cape Hill shows:

Stork Galvanised Iron Works, Tube Works, Monway Iron Works, Patent Brass Tube Works, St George's Works (Screw), Patent Screw Works, Imperial Wire Mills and opposite The London Works Tavern The London Works (Nuts and Bolts): all within 500 yards of each other.

Before crossing the Birmingham Canal at Rolfe Bridge a further nine major concerns are shown as are a myriad of small buildings, wharfs and sheds.

And, of course, there were the pubs, including the London Works Tavern, catering to the needs and thirsts of thousands of workers. Smethwick, in particular, had a heavy industrial base, but a look through the old Ordnance Survey maps of Birmingham and environs show many other enterprises.

Economists, forecasters, wise men, foolish men, ordinary men can all offer reasons as to why we have lost so much manufacturing, why we are unable to compete on price with other countries, why we are better off with our financial and service industries, why cheap migrant labour is necessary, why we are actually very prosperous. Yes, they can and do, but whole communities that made and sold their goods and worked and lived together have disappeared.

GOOD HONEST BEER

The 'tied' house and concern regarding monopoly have been a constant theme throughout this book. After several years of research and recollecting my many, happy times in the 'pub', I am not persuaded that the 'tied' house was wrong. When I consider current monopolies on the High Street and in the Media, I conclude that a vast amount of time, money and effort examining the brewery trade could have been better spent.

It is my firm belief that Henry Mitchell and William Butler created and nurtured a great enterprise that, while it afforded them and their descendants wealth, gave to Smethwick a source of gainful employment, a reasonable quality of life and provided the people of Birmingham and the West Midlands with a good service in pleasant surroundings that would still have its place today. They understood their responsibilities, the inherent dangers connected with their products and, in William Waters Butler, produced a chairman whose work locally and at a national level still commands respect. I have been privileged to meet many who worked for M&B, and I have come across very little evidence of dissatisfaction. No large enterprise can ever be perfect, can ever expect their workforce to be entirely content, but it seems that M&B Cape Hill was, and is, by memory and association, held in great affection.

BIBLIOGRAPHY

The main library in Birmingham with its local archives, press cuttings, and breweries records, allied to the skill and helpfulness of the librarians is an essential source. The Smethwick Heritage Centre has some interesting material relating to M&B and, at the time of writing, I wonder what has happened to the material that used to be stored at the Bass Museum in Burton.

I do not claim that this bibliography is exhaustive, nor would I suggest that all are essential reading, but I have acquired copies of all of them and gleaned something from each and every one.

MAPS: a few maps have been used in the researching of this book. I have listed some below which may be of interest and one essential volume, I suggest, is an up to date

Birmingham A-Z

Old Ordnance Survey Maps: The Godfrey Edition:
Smethwick 1901 Staffordshire Sheet 72:03
Bearwood 1903 72:07
Harborne 1901 13:11
Winson Green 1903 13:04
Birmingham (West) 1914 13:08
Edgbaston 1901 13:12

These are just a few and it is well worth taking a look at others.

BOOKS:

Peter Caddick-Adams: By God They Can Fight! A history of 143rd Infantry Brigade 1908-1995 Shrewsbury 1995

Terry Carter: Birmingham Pals - a history of three city battalions Pen & Sword Books Ltd 1997

Edward Chitham: Harborne, a history. Phillimore 2004

Competition Commission The Supply of Beer for Retail Sale in the United Kingdom 1989 (access via the internet)
                See esp:  Chapter  1 Summary
                         Chapter 12 Notes of dissent

Alan Crawford, Michael Dunn and Robert Thorne: Birmingham Pubs 1880-1939 Sutton 1986

T. R. Gourvish and R. G. Wilson: The British Brewing Industry 1830-1980 Cambridge 1994

Elsie E. Gulley: Joseph Chamberlain and English social politics. USA 1926

Brian Harrison: Drink & the Victorians Keele University Press Revised Ed 1994

J.W. Hartland and K. Davies A History of Cape Hill Brewery 1878-2002 Smethwick 2002

Jess Lebow: The Beer Devotional Adams 2010.
             An American look at beer: a good fun read!

J Parry Lewis: Freedom to Drink Hobart Paper 103 IEA 1985

K H Hawkins A History of Bass Charrington Oxford 1978

Joseph McKenna: Birmingham Breweries Brewin Books 2005

Andrew Maxam: Time Please! A look back at Birmingham's Pubs, based on the M&B archive. Crown Cards 2002

Andrew Maxam and David Harvey: Smethwick (Images of England Series) Tempus 2007

Mitchells & Butler: Fifty Years of Brewing M&B 1929

The Mitchells & Butlers Story: a small pamphlet to be found in the archives at Birmingham Central Library. (They won't let it out of their sight)

Vic Mitchell and Keith Smith: Birmingham to Wolverhampton via Tipton including the Harborne branch Middleton Press 2008

Sydney Nevile: Seventy Rolling Years Faber 1958

Basil Oliver: The Renaissance of the English Public House Faber 1947

Lynn Pearson: British Breweries, an architectural history. Hambledon Press 1999

Ian P. Peaty: Brewery Railways David & Charles 1985

Ian P Peaty: Mitchells & Butlers: a good honest brewery railway.
        (see Railway Bylines Volume 8 no 9 August 2003)

Olive Seabury The Carlisle State Management Scheme. 2007.
Available from: Bookcase 19 Castle Street Carlisle CA3 8SY
Tel 01228 544560 www.bookscumbria.com

Victor Skipp: The Making of Victorian Birmingham Brewin Books 1996

Smethwick Heritage Centre: Smethwick's Industrial Heritage 2008
        Know Your Smethwick 2010

Chris Upton: A History of Birmingham Phillimore 1993

## GOOD HONEST BEER

### BEER PRAYER

Our lager, which art in barrels, hallowed be thy drink.

Thy will be drunk, at home as in the tavern.

Give us this day our foamy head, and forgive us our spillages

As we forgive those who spill against us.

And lead us not into incarceration, but deliver us from hangovers.

For thine is the beer, the bitter, and the lager, for ever and ever,

Barmen

With thanks to Jess Lebow, author of The Beer Devotional.